101 TROUT TIPS

To:

Harry,

Tight Lines,

101 TROUT TIPS

Landon Mayer

HeadWater
Books

STACKPOLE
BOOKS

Published by
STACKPOLE BOOKS
5067 Ritter Road
Mechanicsburg, PA 17055
www.stackpolebooks.com

Printed in the United States of America

10 9 8 7 6 5 4 3 2 1

First edition

Cover design by Wendy A. Reynolds
Cover image by Angus Drummond
Photos by the author except where noted

Library of Congress Cataloging-in-Publication Data

Mayer, Landon, author.
  101 trout tips / Landon Mayer. — First edition.
    pages cm
  Includes index.
  ISBN 978-0-8117-1474-7
1. Trout fishing. 2. Fly fishing. I. Title. II. Title: One hundred one trout tips. III. Title: One hundred and one trout tips.
  QL638.S2M37 2015
  799.17'57—dc23
                        2014027720

Next to Mom and Dad, River Mayer's expression says it all: memories that last a lifetime.

Behind every good man is a great woman! I dedicate this book to my wonderful wife Michelle, who during the highs and lows of life and water is always there. Fly fishing is a way of life for our family, and this book would not be possible without complete love and support. Thank you for everything.

Contents

Acknowledgments

For me fly fishing is a team sport, whether it is teaching others on the water during a guide trip, enjoying the adventure with friends and loved ones, or in this case, creating a visual teaching tool on paper. This project would not be possible without the hard work and dedication of many great friends and individuals on and off the water. I am forever grateful to the following individuals and companies for their support over the years.

I would like to thank my beautiful family, starting with my wife and best friend Michelle and our wonderful children Lauren, Zachary, Madelyn, and River. Sharing the great outdoors with our Brady Bunch is a true blessing. Thanks to my mother Robbie Mayer Skar, and siblings Lauren and Sean.

To Jay Nichols (Headwater Books and Stackpole Books)—our adventures over the years have created some of the most rewarding experiences in all aspects of this great sport. It doesn't even seem like work having so much fun bringing these projects to life. Thank you for everything, my friend!

To Judith Schnell, Tim Gahr, Amy Lerner, Trish Manney, and all the great people at Stackpole Books who make publishing a rewarding and professional experience.

To John Barr, thank you for opening the door early in my career. You are a true friend and a class act for many anglers to follow. The kindness you share with others is what makes this sport grow in a positive light.

To Ross Purnell, Ben Hoffman, and Steve Hoffman for including me in the pages of *Fly Fisherman* and beyond. It is a pleasure being able to share knowledge in such a class act publication. I look forward to more adventures on the water with all of you.

As they say, a picture is worth a thousand words. Matched with the text in this book, I would like to thank Mark Adams, Jack Hanrahan, Pat Dorsey, Bob Dye, Angus Drummond, Mark Lance, Phil Tereyla, and again, Jay Nichols and Ross Purnell for the breath-taking images. It is a pleasure to work with and learn from all of you capturing the right light.

To Joe Mahler, thank you for the great illustrations in this book. Anglers will benefit from the visual learning experience each drawing displays.

To Frank Martin and Jack Tallon. Thank you for your friendship and continued support with *High Country Angler*. I hope to follow in your footsteps to be the best person I can in all walks of life.

A big thank you as well to other great editors I have had the pleasure of working with: Greg Thomas, John Shewey, and Kirk Deeter.

A huge thank you to all the great companies that have supported me over the years, and the wonderful people that make all the great products a reality for so many anglers. It is a wonderful experience helping in design, testing, and promotion for each brand: The MayFly Group with Ross and Abel Reels, Simms, Smith Optics, Umpqua Feather Merchants, Scientific Anglers, Fish Pond, Titan Rod Vaults, and Casio Pro Trek Watches.

To Peter Crow with Smith Optics, thank you for sharing knowledge in text and images in this book for anglers to experience the advantage your lenses supply in all light conditions on the water.

A special thanks to my friend Pat Dorsey. It is has been a pleasure teaching with you on and off the river over the years. Sharing the same passion for our home waters on the South Platte is a true pleasure. I look forward to completing more work together.

It is a pleasure to work with so many top-notch teachers on the water, in the shop, or at club events and shows every year. I look forward to seeing all of you and working toward future projects, giving back to help this sport grow.

Introduction

The fish you land teach you something; the fish you lose teach you everything. Going over losing battles and envisioning a better outcome allows you to become a better fisherman. The basics you learn when you start fishing are a wonderful foundation, but in many cases they are one dimensional.

I want my clients to develop confidence in techniques they once thought impossible and in techniques that go against what they have been previously taught. Fish receive more pressure than ever before, and they adapt by holding in less conventional areas. This is why I felt compelled to write this book. Its outside-the-box mentality and unorthodox approach will help you see the details that can make the difference between a good day and a fantastic day. Each tip presented here starts with a problem, followed by numerous solutions that will help you be successful the next go-round. Sequences of photos accompany the tips because, in my experience, anglers learn best visually both on and off the water. You will see the benefit of thinking beyond the fly and start adapting your approach to both the fish and the water.

PREPARING FOR THE DAY

Preparation for a trip begins before I even arrive at the water. When fishing familiar

Watching Mark Lierz battle this trout of a lifetime was one of the most rewarding experiences of my fly-fishing career. From set to mesh, he applied all the short-game tips we worked on together over the years.

waters, I try to visualize what the water looks like and reflect on past experiences. In new locations, I use a map and satellite images to determine where I think quality trout will be holding; cover, oxygen, and food supply are the trout's most important criteria in choosing feeding lies.

Speed plays a big role in casting to trout in short distances. With the rod in a loaded position, Dave Hoover prepares to present to a hungry target. PAT DORSEY

This mental preparation is similar to an athlete's getting "in the zone." It is almost like you are role-playing how you will fish the water the following day. This can result in extremely positive days.

Before you even consider your equipment, don't overlook the way you dress. Anglers often camouflage themselves to blend in with the river's edge. Because trout see upward in a conical path, it is important to think about what the trout will be seeing above and behind the angler. If your destination is in a canyon, match the canyon walls. If it is fall, match the changing foliage. A bluebird day requires a similar shade of blue.

As for equipment, I usually begin with a nymph rig. No matter what season, weather, or time of day, the odds will be in your favor because a majority of a trout's diet is sub-surface, unless the fish are feeding heavily on the surface when you first get to the water.

Additionally, I rig a second rod with dry flies so I can avoid rerigging if the trout suddenly decide to feed on the surface. Some of the largest trout I have landed were caught during sporadic hatches. In addition to hatches, a break in the weather can allow the trout to feed on the surface, where you can present a hopper or a mouse to trout that have seen nothing but subsurface food all day.

Streamers are tricky. I have yet to meet an angler who can hit the water and nail fish on streamers all day. Streamers work only under specific circumstances. For instance, if the water suddenly increases in flow and becomes off-color, trout will feel much more comfortable attacking large prey. Streamers can also serve as my cleanup method, in which I go back to a previously fished area to present the streamers, hoping wary fish that didn't attack earlier will attack now. No mat-ter what type of water you are on, the last two hours before nightfall bring out the large nocturnal feeders that will take a streamer consistently.

Each discipline of fly fishing will require you to adjust the size of the rod, reel, and line setup. For dry flies I like to use lighter rods and line weights (2- to 4-weight, depending on the water) than I use when fishing nymphs or streamers to add a softer touch to the presentation. A 9-foot rod is ideal for water with room to cast and fish at fair distances. However, if I am fishing pocket waters in tight quarters, shorter is better. Rod lengths from 7 to 8¹/₂ feet prevent snags on waters with heavy vegetation growing from the bank.

The nymphing game has changed over the past five years, with more anglers finding success in waters beyond conventional deep runs or applying tension to the drift. The weight of the setup remains the same for the most part: 4-weights and 5-weights are still some of the most common sizes. In big waters with big fish, like the rivers in Alaska, it is not unheard of to go up to 7- or 8-weight nymph sticks for lifting power. The length of the rods can vary, too. A 9-foot rod will do for most waters and distances. Rods 10 feet or longer do come into play for larger bodies of moving water because they have more reach and fly line control, and on stillwaters because they have more length for lifting and leverage during the fight. If it is feasible, having both a 9-foot stick and a 10-foot stick will cover all water types, from intimate to vast.

For streamers 6- to 8-weight rods are common. I prefer a 7-weight because it is the most versatile, allowing me to fish streamers on a river in the morning and then cast to

Trout see upward at a 45-degree angle when they feed. They see what is above and behind the angler, not what's lining the river's edge. Try to blend in to what is around you and camouflage yourself against the sky, vegetation, or structure. JAY NICHOLS

pike in a stillwater bay in the afternoon. To get maximum power and distance out of a stream rig, try overweighting the rod by one weight in fly line. My preferred set up is a 7-weight rod and reel matched to an 8-weight textured series fly line from Scientific Anglers. The heavier line causes the rod to reach maximum flex and the textured line reduces friction as it shoots through the guides, adding 10 feet (literally!) and speed to each cast when needed.

The reel is one of the most important pieces of equipment you own. It's a misconception that the drag on a reel will not come into play for trout. Yes, some water will allow you to strip line in during the fight. But many of the rivers that I fish have trout strong enough to rip 20 to 30 feet of line off the reel before you can even react, so I prefer large arbor reels with low start-up inertia, a durable build like Ross Reels, and sealed drags to reduce debris entering important moving parts.

When rigging for the trip I always use fresh leaders. Whether you buy them or build them, using fresh tippet will ensure maximum length and strength. After rigging the leader, I check that my tippet spools have at least three feet or more ready for use. I constantly change flies and retie tippets after landing larger trout. I have a tippet spool holder containing X sizes, starting with 0X (for streamers) and continuing up to 3X, 4X, 5X, and 6X. I rarely use 1X or 2X, opting for the strength of 0X instead. For low, clear water, I'll sometimes use 7X, but I prefer sticking to 6X for the strength. Lastly, always double-check your tools for the day, such as strike indicators, fly floatant, knot-tying tools, and markers. There is nothing worse than gearing up or tying on a dry fly and realizing you have no floatant.

After checking my tools I turn my attention to the vise. If you do not tie, concentrate

Without question, the best way to achieve success on the water is through preparation. Having top-of-the-line equipment for all seasons and conditions is the best start. The trout in Thunder Lake, part of Rocky Mountain National Park, did not stand a chance!

on going through and evaluating your fly box. This is the best way to prepare yourself for the trip and develop a systematic plan on how you will present your flies to the trout. I prepare two dozen flies that imitate the predominant food supply in a small container (puck) for easy access while on the stream. I call this being "on deck," akin to a batter getting ready to step up to the plate. I also use this small container as storage for the hot flies. I am a firm believer in speed on the river; yes, you can take the time to organize each fly in its proper place during or after each retie, but you run the risk of missing the few shots you will get at the fish in the process. You can organize your fly box after your trip or before the next day's fishing.

I keep detailed records every month of the year of what the trout are feeding on. If you're just getting started, one of the best books I have found to date is Dave Whitlock's *Guide to Aquatic Trout Foods*. It was my "Bug Bible" when I first started fly fishing. This book is noteworthy for the detailed drawings on each page that show the insect in motion and the format makes it easy to learn.

I carry a core baker's dozen selection of flies with me on the water. With variations in size and color I can match different food supplies throughout the year on most waterways. These flies have proven effective in every season. See "A Baker's Dozen" on page 15.

When selecting flies I try to determine the natural cycle the insects follow throughout a day. These cycles vary with the seasons. The heavy Trico hatch of summer from Pennsylvania to California is an example of this. Many anglers think this small mayfly is only black with spent wings. That version is the most visible insect on the surface as the day approaches high noon, but the hatch starts with the olive-bodied female earlier in the morning. Knowing this is a huge help when presenting a two-fly rig at the beginning stages of the hatch. I start my rig by tying on a traditional black imitation, then trail an olive-body parachute pattern or spinner to match the female. I tie the female as the trailing fly because of how quickly the trout's feeding behavior changes from the

adult female to the adult male. To save time I can change the bottom fly to a spinner and be ready for the next cast without changing my whole rig. I often use this backwards approach, always anticipating the next stage of the hatch.

Weather also plays a big role in determining where you want to start on the river. It triggers fish to move, and most importantly, it makes them either active or lethargic. Tailwaters become the angler's primary target beginning in winter. Unlike stillwaters and freestone rivers, these waterways remain mostly ice-free, with water temperatures hovering around 42 degrees near the dam on most fisheries. This supplies enough warmth to keep trout actively feeding as midges begin to bloom. I always start as close to the dam as possible, knowing that trout from downriver will migrate upstream and accumulate in the deep runs.

In spring the water begins to warm and the stillwaters and freestone rivers start to open. Remember that in this season trout prefer cold water that is warming, making areas like the edges of reservoirs, the inlets to stillwaters, and the lower sections of freestone rivers ideal areas to fish. As in winter, I start my trips near the release of a tailwater or the headwaters of a freestone stream to target active fish. As the temperatures increase, the lower section of the river will become warmer than the cold headwaters or the release from the dam. You can then present your flies to feeding trout in the lower sections of the river during the day.

My favorite areas to search for migratory trout are inlets. As waters warm and open up, large trout begin their migration upriver,

You will see the cloud of male and female Tricos drop to the water's surface. A dual-fly rig with a black male as the lead fly and an olive female trailing below can lead to great results throughout the hatch. JAY NICHOLS

giving you access to large feeding fish. I typically stay away from late spring when these giants begin to spawn. I like the early months of February and March when water temps can drastically increase from early morning to high noon. The river can change from 30 to 40-plus degrees. This temperature swing is enough for a trout to go from a lethargic state to moving and feeding for four hours.

On stillwaters the edge is your best friend, even if the ice has melted away during the preceding weeks. Open water will still cause trout to cruise the edges in search of warm water and food. During low-moisture winters you also want to search the reservoir's inlet. Trout lie in wait for water to move into and

will concentrate in huge numbers. I have seen water levels drop to as low as 30 cfs—too low to allow trout to move upstream. During these conditions, trout from all over the reservoir pile into the inlet area. The urge to migrate and spawn is so strong that the trout won't move around in the rest of the reservoir.

During summer my approach flips. I target the lower and midsections of the river first, knowing they warm quickly. I then move to the headwaters or dam-release areas for cooler water during the midday heat. Finally, I return to the lower or middle section for the last few hours of the day, looking for all species of trout—but most importantly the browns! Fall brown trout and steelhead also prefer warm water that is cooling. This search for ideal temperatures is also important during the summer, when the late hours of the day provide cooler temperatures, in addition to dark water and low light—ideal conditions for the nocturnal predators.

Brown trout and steelhead will begin their migration during the end of summer. This takes place as early as the end of June through July and will sometimes last through December. Brown trout and steelhead migrate farther and longer than other species, making the ability to run early a huge part of the fish's survival. Target the same areas that you would during the summer, but look for more

activity in the low-light hours of the day: early morning, late afternoon, and evening. This is when you'll find the biggest trout.

Daily changes in spring and fall weather can yield good temperatures and produce cover that causes large trout to feel safe and move. Spring snowstorms are good examples of this. When a storm system settles in, the skies are cloudy and the air is insulated, producing warmer water temperatures and increased trout activity. For temperature, it doesn't matter what happens with the skies during the day; it matters what happens during the evening before. In Colorado, clear skies in the evening can lead to below-zero temperatures in the early morning hours of

If you want to target large trout on the feed without the stress of crowds, concentrate on the last two hours of the day. That is when big fish come out of hiding to ambush the next meal.
JAY NICHOLS

the day; the water can take so long to warm that you can run out of daylight for good fishing. If the skies are filled with clouds the night before, early morning air temperatures can start at around 20 to 25 degrees, causing the water to warm quickly and trigger trout activity.

In the fall, daily storms become even more important. The low light caused by dark skies and heavy storms makes fall trout feel comfortable. This is especially true for brown trout, which feed in the evening. Perhaps dark skies fool large trout into thinking that the evening is fast approaching, causing them to feed and move. My favorite four hours of the day are the two before nightfall and the first two hours in the evening. My rule of thumb for the fall night bite is once you see steam rising from the water, the ideal temperatures are nearing their end. Sometimes, you can catch fish until as late as 12:30 a.m.

Finally, clean and store your polarized sunglasses for the day. Polarized sunglasses are an important piece of equipment for hunting trout, defeating glare, and protecting your eyes. When I look back at the times I encountered large trout, many of them were in tough light conditions. These are the hours when big fish can disperse within the river and hunt for their next meal. Time of day, weather, and water visibility are all elements you will battle in pursuit of a trophy fish. If

Without question, quality polarized lenses are one of the most important tools an angler can have. With a comfortable wraparound model, you will eliminate distracting side glare.
JACK HANRAHAN

you do not have the correct lens for the job, you will simply miss seeing the trout. I carry two lenses: brown for midday light because it is dark enough for bright days and light enough for dark days, and a light-colored amber lens for low flat light of early mornings, before dark, and gray storm-filled skies. This will allow more light transfer to see the hunting targets.

When I contacted Peter Crow, manager of Smith Optics, he recommended his company's ChromaPop polarized lenses, which he says will "manage light by blocking confusing light waves, therefore enhancing colors," and Smith's Low Light Ignitor lenses, which "let in ample light during those low-light conditions."

The true chess game begins when you approach the river in your vehicle. The biggest challenge to trout-fishing success is pressure from other anglers. You have to determine where to fish based on how much pressure the trout are receiving, and this depends on the number of cars in the parking lot.

I try to avoid crowded locations. Many people believe that where there are anglers, there is good fishing; I have found the opposite to be true. Targeting the less crowded water in between popular runs is one of the best ways to locate large trout. As fly fishing has become more popular, social media has exposed some of the best runs. Trout are wise in adapting to fishing pressure. They migrate and move to avoid anglers.

Try to find the less noticed areas of the river. Don't worry if the fishing is not at its best where you start, because you should always be on the move. Yes, you could think, "If it's not broken don't fix it," but trout will detect the commotion in a popular run and fishing will eventually slow down. When this happens, be comfortable with moving to new water, especially water that is unfamiliar. This forces you to be more conscientious in how you search and cover the new areas, leading to more success and more good fishing spots.

Once you reach an area where you have a good view of the river from a distance, stop and assess the water and the position of the anglers in front of you. The challenge is now finding less pressured water. I start by identifying stationary anglers in runs, making a mental note of where they are. I can determine later in the day how much pressure these runs have received. This will affect how much time I spend in that section of the river. I pass through heavily pressured water faster than non-pressured water. The second thing you want to look for is anglers walking around, unaware they are spooking trout along the way. I make a mental note of these areas, and usually give the water a thirty-minute rest after it has been walked through or over.

When you guide you become a pointing dog on the hunt all day. Not only am I looking for trout, I am also trying to determine the least stressed water in the river. By navigating the river, fish, and anglers you will be sure to find the best water every time. This is one of the most important keys for locating the largest trout.

With a watchful eye, Mark Adams found some untouched water on the South Platte River during a perfect summer day.

chapter ONE

Fly Selection

By the time I was 10, I was already obsessed with fly fishing. During a camping trip in Colorado's Eleven Mile Canyon, I watched in fascination as anglers consistently landed the trout that had eluded my Zebco-and-Rooster Tail setup. When I was 13 Barbara Pangrack, one of my middle school teachers, would speak to me at great length about her fly-fishing adventures both in the canyon and in many other remote locations.

My weekend job signing people up for subscriptions to the *Colorado Springs Gazette* funded my first equipment from Angler's Covey. One Monday, I witnessed an excited angler ask an employee of the Covey for a specific fly that he had crushed trout on all weekend. The fly was not in stock and the gentleman left empty-handed. Soon after, shop employee and guide Stan Benton leaned over and told me that I should learn to tie so that I would never have to worry about whether a fly was in stock. That summer, to my delight, my birthday present was a fly-tying class with Gary Alameda. While everyone celebrated with a beer after class, I settled for soda.

BANK SHOT

Problem: I keep snagging grass on the river's edge when trying to cast to a feeding fish near the bank.

Solution: Try casting past the bank and allowing the fly to land on the grass. Using a weed guard hopper, you can now twitch the fly snag-free off the bank and into the feeding lane tight to the bank.

Bent-back flies can guard and disguise the hook point, making bank-hugging trout fair game.

think everyone has been there: watching a fish that is sipping adult insects an inch or two off the bank and trying, unsuccessfully, to get the fly close enough so that it actually lands where the trout are feeding—without snagging your fly on the bank. I have had many great casters as clients and some that can make a few curve casts or kick casts, but most of the time their flies don't fall into position.

After considering this problem for a year to find the cure, I discovered that the solution lay in the fly, not the presentation. Now, I add weed or grass guards to many of my dry flies.

I found the best guard is one that extends from the bend of the hook and wraps underneath to the eye. Using fluorocarbon makes the guard less noticeable; in tight quarters on the river's edge, shadows, grass, and foam will prevent the fish from seeing it.

When casting to the river's edge, overshoot your target and land the fly on the grassy bank. Then allow the current to pull the fly line off the bank. Carefully wiggle the rod tip until the imitation falls into the one-to two-inch feeding lane. In many situations the fly will drop off near the target naturally. If you want to extend the drift after the fly hits the water, perform a quick shoot mend upstream after you land the imitation on the grassy bank. The mend will automatically twitch the fly away from the bank, and with the loop of line upstream, you now have an extended drift.

OLD SCHOOL IS THE NEW SCHOOL

Problem: Pressured fish steer clear of the latest and greatest flies.

Solution: Look to the past for time-tested, go-to patterns. These classic ties can yield current results, as the trout have not seen them in some time.

During my early fly-tying lessons, the most important thing I learned, besides the basics, was to tie "old school" without much synthetic material. This forced you to be more disciplined about things like segmentation of the fly, spinning deer hair, and dubbing with wax on thread. I was tying intricate patterns from the beginning and had to pay attention to detail as I tied classic patterns that are now forgotten.

I believe this experience, merged with today's highly effective patterns, has made me more successful in fly selection. I now have a backup plan while trout hunting. What I've found is that often the older pattern with less flash or material is the better fly. The prime example of this is the caddis.

Many caddis larvae look stunning in the bin but fail to perform in the water because they are flashy imitations. Alternatively, the Buckskin is composed of two materials and thread, but because of the chamois leather, it takes on a natural appearance when it gets wet, turning a dull olive or brown. I believe the Buckskin, which is devoid of flash or synthetic material, consistently outperforms most caddis imitations.

It is human nature to look ahead and think about what opportunities await you. This is also true in fly design. But don't forget to look to the past to find a classic, effective imitation. It may seem like something new because it was forgotten by so many. I will often fish two flies at once, with at least one

There are so many flies on the market today that many imitations have been forgotten, especially decades-old patterns like this Woolly Worm. Fish can become conditioned to seeing all the new bugs, ensuring a good reaction—like the one from this Lahontan cutthroat—to time-tested patterns.

drab pattern that has a slim, simple appearance in the water. Go back and research patterns from the 1950s, '60s, '70s, and '80s. Great examples of these are the Buckskin, Hare's Ear, Pheasant Tail, Deer Hair Emerger, and Muddler Minnow.

SEEING RED

Problem: With so many fly color options, it is hard to decide which to use in what season.

Solution: Red is a common attractor for all four seasons.

Trout can be selective when they feed, but large trout will become opportunistic when they are hunting for their next meal because they have to eat constantly to maintain size. A red midge triggered this rainbow cruising near the shoreline at spring ice-off.

With so many fly options, it can be overwhelming and intimidating to find the right one. The number of new synthetics, dyed tying materials, flash, and color changes is constantly growing, making it difficult for anglers to develop confidence in any particular size and color.

I believe, however, that red is almost always a hot color—there is something magical about the color that makes it attractive to large trout. In fact, I am so confident in the color that I carry a red permanent marker with me during all seasons in case I need to color the legs of a hopper in the summer or the body of a pheasant tail in the spring or fall. This is a quick and simple method for getting hookups from aggressive trout.

Fly fishermen often ask, "If you could pick one pattern to have with you at all times, what would it be?" For me the answer is simple—a red Copper John. Since the majority of a trout's diet is below the water's surface, this red imitation can produce during all seasons using all types of flies. It can be the main fly on a dual-nymph rig, a dropper below a favorite hopper, or the lead fly with a chasing streamer behind it.

I will never forget my first trip to New York's Genesee River in 2001. Greg Shelley and I were hoping to feel the tug of big steelhead as these elusive trout migrated up from Lake Ontario. After a full morning without a take, one of the local anglers came down during his lunch break. Sure enough, he landed a huge male tank right in front of us. My initial surprise was replaced by curiosity —what did the steelhead take? While some would only see the Green Egg on the hook, my eyes were instead drawn to the red hook. That night we left the water and began an all-night tying fest. Lo and behold, after a few hours fishing the following day: bam! The first of many Genesee steelhead fell victim to our red-hooked egg.

Adding a red plastic bead to a standard pattern will trigger the trout's aggressive response without overpowering the imitation. I became a fan of adding this element to confidence patterns after seeing how effective Greg Garcia's Rojo Midge has been over the years. I think the fly's red bead is responsible for triggering takes from larger trout.

LEECH LESSON

Problem: Conditions call for a streamer, but mine appears to be oversized in the low, clear water

Solution: Try a smaller leech pattern that mimics the naturals and does not cause trout to become wary of the moving meal.

Anglers can associate the term *leech* with a streamer that is three times larger than a natural leech. While some leeches are large, there are just as many that are an inch long, making the common two-inch leech patterns unrealistic in many circumstances.

I designed the Mayer's Mini Leech to match the small freshwater leeches that trout feed on in big water. This pattern looks like an easy meal to large trout. When the micro pine squirrel is attached near the eye of the hook, the extending material will constantly move, as will the ostrich herl collar. This fly

The best way to determine if your leech imitation is the closest match to the natural is by getting it wet. This lets you see what it will look like below the water's surface as it pulsates through a run.

is versatile; you can dead-drift it as a nymph, swing it as a nymph, trail it behind a larger streamer using a strip retrieve, or even hang it below a hopper. It is also possible to match different colors to the swimming damselflies as they snake their way to the bank. The constant pulsating and undulating action matched with the tapering profile of a leech will fool many trout. It is my go-to pattern for landing large trout in the tight quarters of undercut banks, around structure, and at the head of a drop-off or riffled run. Use this imitation when you are fishing around structure or in tight quarters and want to reduce the number of snags.

STAND OUT IN A CROWD

Problem: My dry fly is getting lost among the naturals during presentations in low light.

Solution: Try changing the color of the imitation, knowing the trout will only see the silhouette in low light.

It can be impossible to see the imitation during the drift amid a blanket hatch of adult insects on the water surface. Selecting flies with bright indicator materials in orange, pink, and red will help you track the fly and see the take. MARK ADAMS

Trout see their prey's silhouette and size when they look up while feeding. Simple, classic imitations like the Griffith's Gnat are the most reliable dry-fly patterns. Once you have selected the right size to match the natural midges on the surface, a common problem is seeing the fly when it is lost in the crowd of natural midge adults.

As a child I was always a big fan of the Orange Asher or Bloody Butcher whenever I fished in new spots, as these flies seemed to work everywhere. I never thought my earliest childhood fishing memories would impart knowledge that would lead to great results in adulthood. By replacing those flies' natural grizzly hackle with dyed pink, orange, or red I was able to track the small imitation in the blizzard of adults and see the take. I have found that pink stands out best in low light.

Using the same bright colors as the post on a parachute dry is another great advantage for trout hunters who want to be able to see their flies in a wide range of light conditions. Select or tie the post dense with material while cutting it low so the fish cannot detect any bright colors on the imitation.

As we do with nymphs, many anglers prefer to fish two dry flies at the same time to give the fish a few options. The dual-dry rigs can really help you track small flies that would otherwise get lost amid the naturals. Unlike nymphs, double drys should be separated by only 6 to 12 inches. From a distance they will appear side by side as they drift downstream. I prefer placing the larger (or tracking) dry first, with the smaller natural imitation trailing behind. Even if the trout does not eat the lead fly, it will appear that way because the lead fly immediately sinks when the rising trout takes the trailing fly.

THE SHRINK CYCLE

Problem: I am using an imitation that matches the natural hatching insect, but I am having poor results.

Solution: Think small when matching the hatch. Trout are less wary of an undersized meal in moving water, even though big meals are the ticket in still waters.

Color and fly pattern are important, but size really matters and makes or breaks your efforts to match the hatch. For river trout that live in the same moving waters year round, you want to think small in fly selection. If your imitation exceeds the natural's size it can put trout on alert. I try to match the size exactly, but if that isn't possible, the safest bet is to downsize by one. This will help you not only make the fly appear natural, but also make the fly mimic the shrinking cycle many insects undergo in river settings.

The best examples of this shrinking cycle are Tricos. When they first bloom in early summer, the insects are at their maximum size, around #18 or #20. The trout watch the size of their meal, and you can get away with larger imitations. As the hatch moves through its cycle from summer into early fall, the insects progressively get smaller, around #22 to #26. This is when downsizing your fly will make all the difference in fooling trout. Because the constant meal of Tricos has been in front of their faces for months, trout are

Even when the water's surface fills with giant insects like Green Drakes, trout are still wary if the imitation is too big. You are better off downsizing the fly to fool selective trout.

aware of the silhouettes' decrease in size and will shy away from anything too big.

For stillwater trout and anadromous fish, insect size changes in reverse. When insects and other food supplies are growing to maximum potential, you want to oversize the fly to get a reaction from cruising trout. A great example of this for stillwater trout is midges, which are known to reach #18 to #14 or even larger. Trout look for these jumbo meals. To induce a take from the trout that are cruising to feed, not holding still like trout in moving water, I will upsize to a #12 midge in the hope that my imitation is more visible to the moving target.

The same principle holds true for migrating trout. When they enter a river system from their deepwater homes they are still used to the food supplies found in the lake or ocean. This can throw river anglers for a loop if they believe that the trout in the river are looking for the small stuff; in fact, if the fish come from a large body of water, they are looking for a large meal.

In addition to insects, migratory trout also eat baitfish, crayfish, and crustaceans. When targeting these trout you can also deliver streamers or other large food imitations that would spook resident trout. Olive and rust are two great colors for matching the look of the baitfish and crayfish that migratory trout eat.

SOFT-HACKLE SUCCESS

Problem: The trout are actively feeding, but they seem to be avoiding my fly.

Solution: Try a soft-hackle imitation that will pulsate in the water, triggering the selective trout to take.

Too often anglers try to mimic a drag-free drift. Soft-hackle flies on a swinging presentation cause the fly to pulsate and undulate, triggering large trout to strike the fly while it is on the move.

As insects begin to move, trout are willing to travel several feet to consume a meal. While you want your fly to mimic the profile of the natural insect, anglers can have problems keeping the trout's attention. In addition to the movement of the fly, drag-free drifts can be difficult for anglers to execute when they are looking for feeding-frenzy behavior.

Soft-hackle flies with materials that give an undulating movement to the imitation will drive fish crazy during heavy hatches of active insects. The best example of this is egg-laying caddis. When the adult caddis dive to the river bottom to lay their eggs they not only leave a bubble trail below the water's surface, but the diving movement becomes the visual cue many trout are looking for. Flies that pulsate while they drift will mimic the natural insect behavior while the line is drifting drag-free.

These flies should be used with swinging or tension drifts that pass through a trout's viewing lane at a 45-degree angle and then disappear to the side. This will often cause the fish to commit. The trout does not want to miss the meal it briefly saw. I have begun tying many classic imitations with a partridge collar, tail, or legs. You can take a simplified pattern and add materials that breathe and move to send trout into a feeding frenzy.

Soft hackle can complement both dry flies and flies that ride just below the surface. Adding a soft-hackle dropper to common emergers will transform them into a real-looking insect emerging out of its nymphal shuck. This is a great way to make a cripple imitation move and get a selective trout to take.

MYSIS: DEAD OR ALIVE?

Problem: I can't decide which *Mysis* to use in high or low water.

Solution: Determine whether the crustacean is alive in high water or dead in low water, and match the pattern accordingly.

On a few Colorado tailwaters, such as the Frying Pan or Taylor, a good *Mysis* pattern is money. With so many *Mysis* shrimp patterns on the market, finding the best one can be problematic. Many lack the movement and color of the natural crustaceans. You need movement from the fly that imitates the natural movement of both live shrimp and dead shrimp. Similar to scuds, shrimp—especially those that are alive—will extend and move horizontally in the water. My *Mysis* (see page 186) is designed on a 200R hook to mimic the natural's length in its profile, and the white ostrich herl on the thorax imitates the active legs of the real shrimp. I tie the antennae out of mini clear legs that wiggle while the current moves the fly. These materials are extremely supple to maximize movement of the fly in water both fast and slow.

In addition to matching movement, you want a fly that can match the translucent look of a *Mysis* that is alive and the opaque color of one that is dead. I prefer to match live shrimp, knowing this is the version most commonly seen by trout.

Mysis are commonly released below different tailwater dams, or swept downstream from the vegetation on the river bottom. In high flow the live shrimp have a chance to drift downstream while remaining alive, possessing a translucent appearance. In low

Always remember that you want two types of *Mysis* shrimp imitations: translucent to match live shrimp and opaque to match dead shrimp.

water many of the shrimp trout see are dead and torn apart from their previous high water journey. These shrimp are opaque, with crippled bodies. An effective but ugly pattern in this situation is a Candy Cane shrimp, size 14-18. Before each adventure to these high-protein fisheries, check flow to match the food supply accordingly.

SINKING FOAM

Problem: I have tried using full-sink lines, but I miss fish from constant snags and vegetation.

Solution: Try using foam flies that elevate your rig above the reservoir or river bottom.

The rewards in deep water are endless when you use foam to ride your imitation just above the bottom of the still or moving water.

One of the best strategies in calm, deep stillwater conditions is fishing streamers with full-sink lines type 2 to 6, using a 7- to 8-weight rod and a foam Pyramid Lake Tadpole (a 2–3 mm foam strip pulled over a cactus chenille body and a trailing marabou tail). This floating fly allows your sinking line to scrape the lake's bottom while the tadpole wiggles a few feet above. You need this deep-end rig because some large fish will find refuge in depths of 30 feet or more right next to shore. This dark environment gives the trout confidence because it can't see movement from above. Using 30- to 60- second intervals (literally look at your watch after you make a cast), or soaks as we call them, will finally get your fly down to the 30-foot zone.

You can find success with this technique in shallower stillwaters and rivers as well. Instead of using the line for sink, tie a heavily weighted fly like Craven's Gonga streamer at the end of a 10- to 15-foot leader, and trail a foam body Woolly Bugger 2 to 3 feet behind the weight. This will keep you presenting near the bottom while the foam streamer rides higher in the column, preventing snags in deep runs or on vegetation in the shallows. In the worst-case scenario, you will at least have the foam fly presenting naturally above the vegetation or structure on the deep bottom.

STICK WITH A BAKER'S DOZEN

Problem: I feel overwhelmed selecting the right fly for each day from my full fly box

Solution: Stick to thirteen core flies that you know work, in various sizes and colors to match the hatch.

Many anglers believe that they need a large array of flies in their box. As many flies are "bin" flies that don't work, this quantity-over-quality mentality becomes an obstacle to success.

After years of guiding and going through hundreds of patterns, I believe the old saying holds true: if it's not broken, don't fix it. Stick to patterns that work, even if they have been around for years. Many of my favorite flies can match different food supplies or be used with numerous disciplines, but they are also easy to tie and don't overdo it on flash or materials. These imitations are versatile flies; by manipulating color and size, you can match numerous hatches and still remain confident on the water. The more confidence you fish with, the better the results.

The best example of a versatile fly is John Barr's Vis-a-Dun. By simply changing the body color, this fly can become a variety of hatch imitations: black imitates Tricos, red mimics Red Quills, olive imitates Blue-Winged Olives, and cahill yellow matches Pale Morning Duns. I just returned from a trip to Pennsylvania to fish Big Spring Creek, Spring Creek, and the Little Juniata River. Like many anglers who prepare for travels, I was trying to find a variety of Sulphur imitations to match the May hatch I was going to encounter. After cranking on the vise and emptying my wallet in the shop, I thought I had my bases covered for flies. As I have encountered so many times before, the ticket for the five days was not the 20 patterns I found, it was a size 14 PMD Barr's Vis-a-Dun,

Barr's Vis-a-Dun is one of the planet's most versatile flies. By changing the body color and size, you can match a Pale Morning Dun on the West Coast and a Sulphur in the East, in addition to a Blue-Winged Olive or a Trico—all with just one pattern.

proving to me again some flies can do the job nationwide! Great fly fishers carry a selection of twelve to thirteen in various colors and sizes. Size and color are the two most important considerations in fly selection; changing just these two things while using the same fly can lead to success.

Here are thirteen patterns I like to use:

1. #6-12 Meat Whistle (ginger, rust, olive)
2. #10-12 Lawson's Conehead (sculpin, black, olive)
3. #14-18 Micro San Juan Worm (red, earthworm brown, pink)
4. #14-16 Mayer's Mini Leech (black, brown, olive)
5. #16-20 Copper John (red, green, black, zebra)
6. #18-22 Tube Midge (red, black, copper)
7. 4mm McFly Foam Egg (orange, cheese, apricot)
8. #16-18 Mayer's *Mysis*
9. #12-22 Flashback Pheasant Tail
10. #16-22 Craven's Juju (Baetis, PMD)
11. #16-20 Barr's Vis-a-Dun (Green Drake, Red Quill, BWO, PMD, Trico)
12. #16-20 Puterbaugh Caddis (black, brown, gray body)
13. #16-20 Buckskin

THE FORGOTTEN FLY

Problem: The trout are so selective that they have refused all my variations of the adult.

Solution: Try a terrestrial imitation that doesn't match the current hatch to trigger a take.

I never leave a selective trout that is rising to everything except my flies. Ants often get wary fish to rise. Make sure the ant matches the size of the natural insect you were imitating before.

When dealing with selective trout feeding on the surface, many anglers start changing dry flies to find out what the fish will take while still matching the hatch. There are some trout, however, that simply will not commit to a meal that looks like it might escape.

To solve this problem, think beyond the hatching insect and go with one or two imitations that mimic a food supply that does not start from a hatch. I call them the "forgotten flies," referring to ants and beetles. These food supplies fall, fly, drop, or are blown into the water. They are my go-to cleanup flies that seem to always get a rise from trout that simply will not take a hatch-matching imitation. While ants and beetles come in a variety of colors, I find that black is the best and most versatile selection for all waterways.

My go-to pattern is usually the ant—not just a normal ant, but the flying ants that are found on a waterway during specific times of the year. I think it appears more natural to a trout when there is a wing case extending slightly past the butt section of the body. This way it matches an ant that lands on any portion of the river, not just the edge.

THE GARDEN BURGER

Problem: The flows just increased, tinting the water, pushing chunks of vegetation and debris downstream, and slowing down the bite.

Solution: Try matching the color of vegetation with a suitable imitation.

It's a visual that sounds far-fetched if you haven't witnessed it, but once you do, matching the hatch will take on a vegetarian quality. I am referring to trout pursuing small patches of vegetation for a meal, knowing that green, tan, or brown clumps are full of insects, dead or alive, for the fish to eat. I first saw this on the San Juan River in 1999, when a local angler showed me a fly that honestly resembled a small leech and said he'd been killing it on the fly all week. After his helpful conversation in the parking lot, I tied his generous donation on as my main fly. The morning was filled with great battles from fish willing to chase the pine squirrel fly numerous feet to strike.

While presenting flies to the fish, I also noticed small clumps of almost identical veg-etation drifting down stream. Then, to my surprise, I watched the same fish I was hunting race over and eat the vegetation. Some would swallow it whole, while others chewed on it like an oversized piece of gum before spitting it out. In the afternoon I took the time to sift through handfuls of vegetation on the river bottom, and then the light bulb went off. It was packed with midges that the trout had located as a platter of food.

I have continued to use this technique on numerous waterways with great success. If, when flows increase or are flowing higher than normal, you match the vegetation color by selecting a small (1 to 2 inch long) leech with no flash, the trout will be searching for the next big clump drifting below the water's surface. This imitation is versatile, taking on an appearance of a small fry darting around the river's edge, clumps of flesh that detach from the rotting carcass of a salmon, and, of course, leeches that attach to vegetation and rocks along the river's bottom. Trout are masterful at adapting how they eat and where the food comes from, and a small leech imitation covers several of these potential food sources.

HIGH-WATER ATTRACTION

Problem: I am used to fishing worms in high flows, but my fly is not working in the dirty water.

Solution: Try a leech, scud, or sow bug—types of food that trout also see in high water.

Anglers can see high water and immediately assume their attractor pattern should consist of a worm. While this can be true, these anglers are neglecting other patterns that can be much more effective.

Worms are most effective when high flows have just begun and previously dry banks are newly flooded so that worms are escaping into the water. At this point the water is dirty. Always make sure you take the time to try different worm imitations, like micro chenille, wire worms, and a new but very effective supple material, Squirmy San Wormy. These variations of the worm will drift differently and achieve high and low depths within the water. Once the high water clears, leeches, scuds, crane flies, or sow bugs are more effective as trout come out of their comfort zones to investigate the attractor.

Also consider coloration of these food sources by examining vegetation, wood structures, or the river bottom for the real meal you're imitating. Leeches are often olive, black, or brown; scuds, tan or olive; crane flies, tan or olive; and sow bugs are often gray. One of my favorite high water rigs is a lead fly consisting of a leech, scud, or sow bug, followed by a dropper Barr's Crane Fly Larva. This heavy fly looks the part and becomes the main weight, making deep tension drifts a realty in the most turbulent of waters.

HOT LEGS

Problem: The fish are literally bumping my hopper out of the way to not eat it.

Solution: Try a hopper imitation with brightly colored legs.

Most hopper imitations lack color in key places such as the legs. They instead concentrate on placing the color on the body, making the legs dull. While these imitations can be successful, real hoppers usually have color on their legs. On my home waters of the South Platte, the hoppers have bright red legs, and I have seen others with deep blue. Catching hoppers and examining their legs can tip you off to a color that you can tie or buy that may trigger more interest from the trout.

It is also wise to carry a red permanent marker so that you can color the legs of purchased flies. This trick, which we've already used for enhancing some egg patterns, can provide you with that extra edge. When you do take to artistry on the legs of your fly, concentrate on the two hind legs. As seen in the photo at right, that is where the color is located, and these legs are fully extended and visible when hoppers ride on the water's surface.

When selecting hoppers make sure that you choose patterns that ride low in the water, with the legs extended out and behind to the side. Naturals usually have spread legs and their bellies are submerged.

It was a true surprise when I flipped this hopper over on the river's edge and found blue legs. The key is matching the bright color of the natural's legs, which are all trout will see from below the surface.

chapter TWO

Ready to Rig

In 2001, a talk by John Barr at the Peak Fly Shop's Rep Day flipped a switch in my head. As John described his Hopper Copper Dropper rig, I started to understand the importance of starting light, or high in the water column, and working my way down through different depths, allowing a trout to naturally lift and feed. It dawned on me that anglers, lacking confidence in topwater and subsurface presentations, go too deep too fast.

On my next guide trip, I began having my clients fish different rigs. I had one fish a Hopper Copper Dropper and had the other fish a standard nymph rig of two flies, split shot, and a strike indicator. It was amazing how many fish not only reacted to the natural appearance of John's rig, but were willing to rise to the higher fly no matter what the season.

This forced me to constantly make adjustments to rigs during guide trips. Instead of being a cumbersome chore, it became part of my clients' daily routines. The results were phenomenal. I began to learn more about trout's feeding patterns for drys, nymphs, and streamers. Clients began having more success in hookups and left with more knowledge.

While fishing in Alaska in 2009, I watched J. B. do it again. We made an opening-week trip to Clearwater Lodge on the Kvichak River, known for its big rainbows that migrate in from Lake Iliamna to chase. We tried various presentations, from swinging egg-sucking leeches with a switch rod to nymphing pegged beads, all with limited success. J. B. made an adjustment to his rig that changed the whole game. As J. B. is the only angler I have known who fishes exclusively with his own patterns, he did what came naturally: he switched his rig from a conventional nymph style to a rig that used his natural-colored Jig Slumpbuster connected to a 9-foot 3X leader that was suspended 5 feet below a strike indicator. Much to everyone's surprise, the next three drifts produced three beautiful, fat, chrome rainbows.

Everybody gets lazy when it comes to rigging. The best way to combat this is to continue thinking outside of the box and to try new rigs even in the worst weather conditions. A great example of this is in the "X-factor" tip on page 32. It allows you to control every step of knot tying, even in 30-mile-an-hour winds when it is 10 degrees outside. When changing rigs becomes second nature, your perspective and performance will evolve.

DOUBLE-FISTED

Problem: I am spending too much time re-rigging, causing me to miss the hatch or the calm conditions when the fish feed.

Solution: Bring multiple rods on the river with you to match different conditions.

With high flows on the Little Juniata River in central Pennsylvania, Jay Nichols and I prepared for the day, double-fisted with nymphs and streamers. Using both streamers and nymphs at the same time, our reward was two quality browns right off the bat. JACK HANRAHAN

Constantly changing flies or knots is a pain. It sometimes results in missing the hatch and, subsequently, the topwater bite. Having to change your rig from dry flies to nymphs, or nymphs to streamers, can slow down your pace enough to affect the day's success. You've also got to worry about bad knots resulting from shaking hands as you see and hear a rising fish taking drys while you're stuck changing a nymph rig.

Bringing two or more rods to the river will help you overcome this and be ready for the changing river conditions. One rod can be rigged with duns or cripples, one with cripples or spent, and, if you have enough toys (i.e., rods and reels), a third with spent or sunk. You can then reel up and set one rod down, allowing you to simply grab another and cast to new targets in no time. I live by this method as a full-time guide. I need to make sure that no opportunities go unnoticed and give my clients the best shot at success. This method is so effective that I rarely leave home without at least two rods available. Another advantage to this setup is having drys, nymphs, and streamers ready for action.

I start with drys to see if I can get a fish to rise, or I target rising fish. I switch to nymphs when the hatch slows down or when the adults have laid their eggs, died, and been swept down below the water's surface. This is when the next hatch begins to rise, or when the subsurface food supply is the trout's main target. Finally, I will use streamers as my cleanup rig. Because they create the most disturbance on the surface, I use them last. By following this progression, I will know I gave it my all. If I could only have one rig, it would be nymphs because more than 80 percent of a trout's diet is subsurface.

LEADER DIAMETER CONTROL

Problem: The trout are getting spooked by my rig.

Solution: Try building your own leader with long pieces of thinner diameter.

Anglers struggle with wary trout not detecting their rigs in clear-water situations. I think this has to do with the diameter of the leader they are using and how it moves below the surface. Most trout leaders are thinnest around their last two feet, tapering down from the thick butt section of the material.

I learned how effective building your own leader was when I guided on Alaska's Naknek River in 2003. Not only was building leaders cost-effective, I could also have less drag in the water as my flies drifted downstream, thus decreasing the chances of a fish seeing the leader. I recommend taking a standard 9-foot, 5X fluorocarbon leader and cutting it back to near four feet. Instead of retying a piece of 5X tippet, tie a piece of 4X tippet to replace the lost leader material. The advantage is the strength you gain from going up to 4X; cutting away two feet of the thick taper makes it harder for trout to detect. This eliminates the need to go down to a weaker 5X tippet.

The same setup also works in topwater conditions with rising trout because there are fewer disturbances from the thin diameter on the water surface; it does not reflect as much light, and it makes for more natural drifts, with less drag below the water's surface. For really wary trout, you can add five or six feet of a straight-running tippet to give you more distance to reach the wary rising target.

LEADER ID SYSTEM

Problem: I can't tell how deep my rig is to find the right feeding depth.

Solution: Try marking your leader every few feet to be precise on depth control.

Place the tip of a black, brown, or green permanent marker on the leader where you want to identify the depth. I apply one mark every three feet; a 9-foot leader has three marks. Once you place the tip of the marker on the leader, with your opposite fingers gently roll the leader forward. This will make a clean strip around the diameter of the leader.

There is a lot of guesswork that goes into fly fishing, especially when it comes to rigging and the length of leaders and tippets. With experience you can excel at eyeballing distance for a proper setup, but I have found that being off by even six inches can make or break your presentation and cause problems when sight-fishing in tight quarters or deep water.

After numerous encounters with stillwaters or deep runs where trout were staging, I quickly realized that even a veteran eye could miss its mark and misjudge the correct depth for the best presentation. I then started marking my leaders every three feet with green or brown permanent marker. I prefer brown because it is less noticeable in deep water but remains darker above the surface, making it easier to see. Simply start three feet below the end of the leader and mark one strip for three feet, then make another mark after another three feet. Continue this to the end of a 9-foot leader, and you will have three strips marked at the bottom.

When you are kicking around a lake and you or your fishing buddy hook up, your depth should be the first thing you determine. Once trout determine at what depth they are going to feed in stillwater, they simply swim in search of the next meal. If you are above or below that feeding line you will miss takes. By using the leader marks, you can quickly lift your leader and judge its length. It is easier to eyeball distance in three-foot increments, compared with judging an entire nine- or twelve-foot leader.

NIGHTTIME INDICATORS

Problem: I can't see my indicator at night.

Solution: Make your own indicator with glow sticks and slip indicators.

For years I attempted to find the right indicator for fishing at night. Suspending flies during the evening hours is important because you cannot see the depth of each run and you want to prevent snags that would result in losing your rig. I tried colored indicators, regular yarn, and glow-in-the-dark yarn. My latest experiment was with glow-in-the-dark indicators, which required charging the chemical on the indicator with artificial light. It proved ineffective because the indicator lost its charge in cold water, and I was only able to get a few drifts. I also ran the risk of spooking large trout with the bright light necessary to charge the indicator.

The wonderful thing about guiding anglers from around the world is how much new information you receive. True harmony comes from a trip in which you supply your client with information, while learning from the client as well. If you always keep your mind open, you will learn something new every day on the water. This was true for one client from Missouri. He was an avid angler on Lake Taneycomo, where the night bite is a part of daily fishing. After I expressed my frustration in trying to find a nighttime indicator, he gave me the key!

His rig was genius. It was not only bright enough for tracking purposes, it was long-lasting. You can use it for hours on end. Start with a medium white slip indicator. Apply the indicator by sliding it onto your leader before attaching flies or tippet material. Once you find the right location on the leader, peg the indicator with the plastic insert that comes with it. Replace the plastic insert with a small glow stick of the same diameter. (You can find these at sporting goods stores like Bass Pro Shops and Cabela's.) This inch-long glow stick will stay illuminated for hours after the chemicals react when you snap the stick to make it glow. When inserted, the glow stick will ride horizontal on the surface and light up the white indicator, making it visible for every drift.

A luminescent line used instead of an indicator can be a fantastic tool, so long as you keep in mind that you don't overcharge the line to the point of spooking fish. When used with a leader, you can see the entire presentation at night.

Illuminated indicators that require exposure to a light source before use are known to lose light when exposed to cold water. Using a mini glow stick as the insert in a foam strike indicator will keep you in visual contact with your rig for hours, if not all night long.

INDICATING INVISIBLY

Problem: I need a low-maintenance indicator that I can see but which does not spook wary trout.

Solution: Try a no-maintenance plastic see-through indicator.

The clear Thingamabobber in sizes small, medium, and large is almost invisible when drifting over wary trout. It mimics the dirty translucent water bubbles that are found all over the river.

Yarn is difficult to cast, maintain, and keep undetected from trout. While yarn is more sensitive, it can also cause anglers to become overpowering with their mends and line control because it sits wet in the water's film, with less movement.

The number one reason I use see-through or glow-in-the-dark Thingamabobbers is that they are virtually invisible to trout when drifting overhead. A see-through indicator creates no contrast against the sky for trout to see. The clear or white Thingamabobbers become invisible in foamy water. In addition to changing the color, you can change the sizes to further prevent trout from detecting you. I have found that trout are wary of large objects drifting overhead because they are accustomed to predator threats from above.

This indicator is also easy to cast compared to yarn, which causes an incredible amount of wind resistance. By simply switching from large to medium, or medium to small, this small-diameter plastic ball can cut through the breeze. This is important in windy conditions, when casting even short distances is a challenge. I am also a fan of presenting flies using a straight line from rod tip to indicator for accuracy. A small Thingamabobber can easily cut through this wind. Lastly, indicators can cause tension and drag in certain water speeds. The larger

the indicator, the more unnatural drift you can achieve because the leader is pulled by the surface of the water. Changing from a medium to small Thingamabobber takes only seconds, and can allow you to defeat drag on the surface of the water.

Depth control is one of the keys to success in any trout environment. Your flies should drift into the fish's viewing lane at the correct depth in the water. I can rely on the buoyancy of a Thingamabobber for all sizes of flies without maintenance during the day.

If you applied the same mending power using a Thingamabobber, you would end up lifting the indicator out of the water with each mend. This is nice because you become more efficient with each mend and create fewer disturbances on the water's surface.

WORK DOWN TO THE FISH

Problem: I can't tell what depth to fish at.

Solution: Try a tier system to replace split shot or putty.

Anglers can feel overwhelmed when faced with different water speeds and depths, especially in dark-water conditions. A systematic approach can lead to greater success. Many experienced anglers develop a tier system when applying split shot or tungsten putty to their rig. I prefer starting light and then, if needed, adding more weight to achieve depth. This allows the trout to lift in the water column to take the fly without you

spooking, rubbing, or snagging the fish by starting with too much weight. It is true that the difference between a good and an advanced angler is one split shot, because you are making constant adjustments to achieve the right depth. Trout have become so selective now that this traditional method of achieving depth with split shot or putty can be enough to spook wary trout, as it appears to be an unnatural object drifting by.

Eric Mondragon pulls over to secure a fresh depth rig for rising trout on the Missouri River in Montana. When facing a variety of shallow- and deepwater conditions, achieving the right depth is key using subsurface flies. If you have not experienced the selective nature and intense power of a "Mo Bow" (Missouri River rainbow) you are missing out.

To prevent this, you can develop the same tier system with tungsten or plastic beads on your flies to achieve depth without shot. For example, if you tie a #18 Pheasant Tail you can use a $1/8$-inch, $3/32$-inch, or $5/64$-inch tungsten bead to achieve numerous depths mimicking the use of #2, #4, or #6 split shot. This is ideal for deep water scenarios where you are achieving depth without snagging the river bottom. In shallow water, typically three feet or less, tungsten beads can be too much weight, making plastic beads in sizes x-small, small, and medium the best option for drifting your flies without snagging river bottom before they reach the trout's viewing lane.

When you are presenting in deep water, you want the trailing fly to be the heaviest, allowing you to drift close to the river bottom while the unweighted lead fly is drifting above, covering numerous feeding depths. In shallow water, you want a weighted lead fly and an unweighted trailing fly, giving your drift a more horizontal movement. This technique will increase the amount of hookups you achieve each day by making your rig appear as natural as possible.

SETTING THE TENSION

Problem: After the fight begins, the fish breaks off during a quick run.

Solution: Set your drag at home before hitting the river and leave it in place.

When fighting trout, an angler will often change the tension setting of the drag during the fight. Yes, this can apply more pressure, but overadjusting can cause the trout to break off. When you are moving around and fighting trout in the heat of the battle, it is difficult to make an adjustment by turning the tension dial on the reel's drag setting.

I am a firm believer that once your drag setting is placed, you should leave it be. I never change the drag setting on my reel. You want the drag to allow line to be reeled whenever there is power applied by the trout during the fight. This typically occurs during the fish's runs or headshakes. The drag will release line before the rod is fully flexed, preventing the full pressure from being transferred to the tippet, which would cause the trout to break off. You want to have a maximum flex (bend) of the rod without line releasing; this allows you to apply power and causes the fish to headshake.

The first method of setting a drag properly can be done in the comfort of home. Connect the leader or fly line to a chair with a simple overhand knot. Using a convex bend, lift your rod until you reach a full bend without the line being released. This is the same bend you will have on the water, the one that causes the trout to headshake and

Hunting for chromers (fresh fish that have not been in the river long) is the goal for anglers who know the stronger the fish, the harder the fight. With proper tension set on his drag, Angus Drummond won the fight against this Pilot Peak-strain Lahontan cutthroat.

tire out quickly. The key is maintaining this bend without line releasing from the drag until the fish makes a power motion with its body. Tighten your drag at the full bend to the point that line does not release. Make small lifting motions about one foot in length, adjusting the drag so line is released with every quick lifting motion. This is similar to the movement you will feel when a trout headshakes during the fight. The drag prevents you from reaching the breaking

point while still allowing you to apply maximum pressure during battle.

If you have to make an adjustment on the water you can use the same technique, or, if you are with a fishing partner, have him or her hold the line and simulate the same movements. Pull line down to imitate the headshake, or quickly pull back three to four feet to imitate the fast run of a fish. Both techniques will allow you to determine the proper reel setting, allowing the reel to do its job and perform correctly on the water.

SLIDING EGGS

Problem: I can't seem to use eggs and streamers effectively because the trout are not willing to take an egg-sucking leech.

Solution: Try a sliding egg rig.

In the spring and fall large trout switch their diet from primarily insects and the occasional large meal to one that contains more eggs. Their willingness to chase down large food is the trout's reaction to the heavy pre-spawn aggression. For years I tried to combine eggs and streamers in one rig, with some success. The problem was the constant separation of the two food supplies. I needed the egg to appear as if a smaller baitfish "streamer" was eating it during the retrieve.

I decided to try a sliding method for the egg above the streamer so that every time the rig was drifting without a retrieve the egg would separate from the streamer by a few inches. With every strip, the egg would con-

nect to the eye of the hook, giving the rig the awesome lifelike appearance of a baitfish attempting to eat an egg as the rig swings through the run. It is one of the best ways to trigger a strike from large trout.

To set up the rig, use a 10-inch piece of 1X or 0X tied to the eye of the streamer with a clinch knot. Slide a 4mm apricot-orange egg bead onto the tag end. With the remaining tag end, make a blood knot that connects the tag end to the leader. When the blood knot is complete you will have two tag ends that need to be cut close to the finished knot. Cut one close and leave the other tag end a quarter inch in length. This small tag will prevent the egg from sliding past the bite tippet and allow it to move with your presentation.

Some tungsten beads can replace eggs. The sliding bead acts as weight control. There is also an indentation at one end so that when the bead rides close to the streamer or hook it looks more natural as it hides the eye.

THE X FACTOR

Problem: I am having trouble rigging during adverse weather.

Solution: Try the X factor, controlling each step of the knot.

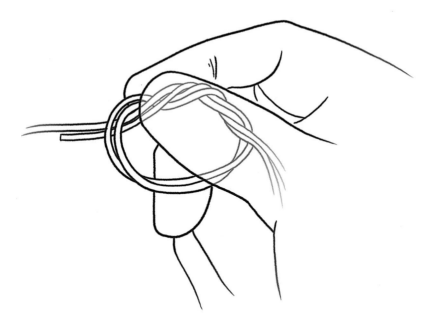

When the tag ends of the leader and tippet cross you see an X. Pinch the X with your fingers keeping control of each step while rigging. After practice, you will be able to rig quickly and perform the knot without even looking at your fingers. JOE MAHLER

One of the best ways to fool wary trout is by constantly changing and adapting your rig. The problem for some is how long it takes to rig and, in rough conditions like wind, all it takes is a big gust of wind to make the knot unravel, forcing you to start all over again. And if you take too long to rig, you could find yourself sitting on the bank in the thick cloud of a quick hatch and missing all the action.

Without question, practice—both on and off the water—makes perfect when performing knots. There is also another trick that allows you to have control of the knot during every step; I call it the X factor. Every time there is an X in the knot from both tag ends crossing, you will pinch on the X and maneuver the tag ends to place them through the knot until it is complete. The best knot to use as an example is the triple surgeon's knot.

Start with two short tag ends about two inches in length and place them on top of one another. Then get the material moist with some saliva. Next, coil the materials with the tag ends taut in your thumbs and index fingers of both hands. This will create a circle with an X of the crossing tag end at the top. With your right or left thumb and index finger, pinch on the X and let the tag end on both sides go. From here place the long tippet tag end and the short leader tag end behind your thumb and index finger. This will place the tag ends behind and in the middle of the circle, allowing you to pull them through with your opposite thumb and index finger. Repeat the process until you have gone through the loop three times, performing a triple overhand (surgeon's) knot. The great thing is that the X factor can be used for any rigging knot.

THE RIGHT NIGHT LIGHT

Problem: I am spooking fish at night with a powerful spot light.

Solution: Try a red head light.

I find the problem facing nighttime fly fishers is trusting the bite in the dark. Instead of being subtle about how much light they use, many anglers use bright illumination to spotlight the fish below the water's surface, or on the river's edge. Yes, you will see great action and big fish. You will also witness fish spooking out of their nighttime feeding locations. You want to avoid overusing light.

Think of what you *need* to illuminate: your chest area for knot tying and the ground or river's edge for safe wading. This light should also extend to the river's edge, giving you a little encouragement in where you are presenting the flies. The best color is red to preserve the angler's night vision, and not attract the bugs that could obstruct your view. Large trout become nocturnal predators

This 23-pound male brown trout is a prime example of why I never use less than 0X when rigging streamers in the dark. It is not uncommon to see giants like this with half-inch fangs.
PHILLIP TEREYLA

because they have the safety of dark cover. Interrupt this cover and you take away the main reason trout hunt at night in the first place.

Another way to use an ordinary spotlight is to use the halo around the main middle beam. This will keep the bright main beam away from the trout, while the outside halo is bright enough to see more trout without destroying their cover.

THREE

Timing is Everything

In 2002, an older gentleman I was guiding on a Colorado Fishing Adventures trip told me that there are two things an angler will talk about at the end of every day: how many fish he caught, and how big the giant really was. My client also stated that as you mature on the water you will begin to challenge yourself with not only catching larger trout, but also with trying to find where these giants are hiding. Boy was he ever right!

About a year later, I received a phone call from Matt Bynum, a friend and fellow guide who was working at Naknek Anglers in Alaska. He had injured his back and was going to be out for the season, and they needed a full-time guide at their lodge in King Salmon. I was thrilled to accept, even though they expected me there in three days! I was in for a challenge in one of the planet's biggest migratory waterways. Little did I know at the time, but this experience would shape how I time trips to any waterway: I target the migra-

tion beyond the spawn, the same period when most anglers time their trips.

I was first clued in to this as I sat down with the head guides and watched them coat plastic beads with three coats of paint to mimic the different stages of an egg's exposure to the water. As I listened to them call home looking for a specific color of nail polish, I realized that we were hunting trout based not on the trout's migration to spawn, but their migration to feed. The trout our clients caught had come hundreds of miles to eat eggs and flesh from the carcasses of the salmon. I spent the next fourteen weeks learning how predatory trout truly are and brought this knowledge back with me to the lower forty-eight.

I now thought not only in terms of the trout's spring and fall spawning migrations, but also the feeding migrations that they make on a daily, weekly, and seasonal basis. For example, during August, brown trout will hide under cover in the heat of high noon. At dusk, when the temperatures have cooled, these fish migrate to shallow waterways or the river's edge to pursue crayfish or mice. Migrations don't have to be thousands of miles; they can be only thousands of feet.

I think that far too often anglers book trips months or years in advance based on a narrow pre-spawn window, when a broader time frame and flexible schedule can result in less pressured waters. The best trips I have had on waterways across America have come from unconventional thinking like this.

With a bloom of Indian paintbrush at his feet, Gary Hort marched on with confidence that stoneflies were on the trout's diet.

THE EARLY BIRD DOESN'T ALWAYS GET THE WORM

Problem: I am showing up early and having limited success.

Solution: Try showing up during later hours when you know the hatch takes place.

This is a close-up shot of one of the most effective West Coast meals to imitate at high noon during the heat of summer, a Pale Morning Dun. The key to success is choosing the right color, melon or yellow. This dun was one of many sailboats that day.

It is an old saying: "The early bird gets the worm." In our context, it means the first angler to the river will be rewarded with the best water to fish and the best fishing to unpressured trout. While it is true that you will find fewer anglers about, especially in cold or stormy conditions, the problem is that early anglers miss some of the best action the river can supply because the water temperature needs to increase for hatches to bloom and trout to become active. I usually start my trips between eight-thirty and nine in the morning. No, I am not being lazy—I am targeting water that is full of activity and not wasting the angler's time when the fishing is slow.

Start timing the hatches you see and fish, and take notes for future reference. This will help you understand when to be on the water. It also helps to take the temperature of the river every time you see a hatch come off or fish begin feeding. Having this reference is key because the weather is never the same; some years are colder or warmer than others, and this can affect trout behavior.

By starting at nine o'clock in the morning, I am able to see what food supplies are active in the afternoon hours. Some anglers leave as the first hatch dies, but the trout are simply waiting for the next meal. I see this a lot in my home state of Colorado. The Tricos bloom in the morning hours, producing great dry-fly action. This hatch will begin to disperse by noon, fooling many anglers into thinking the hatch is done and it is time to leave. By one o'clock in the afternoon the Pale Morning Duns begin to hatch and the action starts again. Never cut yourself short from action, and don't lose quality time by leading the hatch too much in the morning.

FOLLOW NATURE'S CLOCK

Problem: I can't seem to time the hatch on a specific river.

Solution: Try keeping a detailed journal, remembering that it will change year to year based on water temperature.

Timing a hatch can be as easy as setting your watch to the same time every day for a few months, or as difficult as fishing a specific river year after year and finally—after five years—hitting the hatch in its prime. The problem with timing the hatch is that anglers get attached to dates and not weather or water conditions.

To have the best chance at predicting a hatch on any river, take water temperature readings and write down notes describing the day's conditions. Was the water high or low, clear or dirty? Were the skies clear or cloudy? Was it raining or snowing? This info will let you know what conditions are needed for the hatch to go into full swing. Then next year you can look at the water flow and weather conditions and say, "Oh yeah, it should be good based on my notes," or "Wow, it may be a few weeks until the hatch pops." A great example of this occurs during the "Mother's Day Hatch" on the Arkansas River. What many anglers fail to realize is that some years this is actually a "Tax Day Hatch" that can be enjoyed without as much angler pressure.

One of the best clocks for an angler to live by is Mother Nature. On my home waters of the South Platte River I keep a close eye on the bloom of wildflowers, knowing the hatch will blossom at the same time. Purple irises mean caddis are here.

I also think that we should look at hatches in a different light and consider what's below the water's surface. Yes, what we see is on top of the water. And yes, topwater fishing can be the most exciting way to fool a trout to eat—but don't cut yourself short. The bugs that land on the water and die eventually sink below the surface, causing a feeding frenzy unseen by most anglers. This subsurface feeding can lead to great results. Or how about the emerging insects that are on their way to adulthood? The movement of the insects prior to the hatch can also trigger a feeding frenzy before the visible hatch. Lastly, remember that the hatch does not always occur during a single day. Caddis and stoneflies, for example, move below the surface a month or weeks before they hatch. This will trigger a feeding response from the trout and allow you to keep the same flies on your rig for a month at a time.

Use blooming flowers or other vegetation as indicators of the timing of a particular hatch. The water and air temperatures that produce the blooms can also bring about the food source you are looking for. In Colorado, purple irises blooming are an indication that the caddis are in season, while the presence of Indian paintbrush can mark the stonefly season.

WEEKENDS ARE THE NEW WEEKDAYS

Problem: I want to avoid crowds on the river.

Solution: Try fishing on the weekend—often everyone else is avoiding it.

With so many anglers getting into the sport of fly fishing, avoiding crowds becomes part of a successful day. Timing the trip to find less pressured trout is key. Unlike this photo, I always try to give anglers at least fifty feet of water to explore up- or downstream. JAY NICHOLS

Many think that weekends are always overcrowded and not worth the hassle. A lot of anglers have work or other activities that keep them tied up during the week, forcing their time on the water to fall on the weekend. All it takes is one experience on the water during a crowded weekend, when the trout have simply had too much pressure

and stop feeding, to sour an angler on weekend fishing.

This has been going on for so long that reverse psychology is now playing a role. The weekends have become the new weekdays for a good number of my guide trips. Everyone believes that they are escaping the crowd of the weekend by hitting the water during the week. This has resulted in less pressure on the weekends, giving trout a chance to feed. Even when anglers see more pressure during the weekdays, they will have an excuse for the crowds and think that another weekday will be better. Some are simply not willing to believe that the weekend is the answer in some environments.

Time your trip around when you see anglers leaving, not when you see them arriving. It is incredible to see how many anglers leave in early afternoon at the first threat of a thunderstorm. I find that there are fewer anglers and more activity later in the day after a storm and reduction in barometric pressure.

MICE BITE

Problem: There is too much glare in the early evening to fish.

Solution: Try a big meal, like a mouse. Rely on the surface contrast between fly and glare to see the rise.

Glare has always been an enemy of anglers. But as they say, keep your friends close and your enemies closer. Anglers should heed that advice and apply it to glare. Yes, glare makes it impossible to see beyond the water's surface, but it can make the same surface a tracking device for some of the most exciting dry flies in the world— like mice.

During the first or last two hours of the day, when the glare has created a mirror of clouds on the water's surface, use the movement or drift of a mouse to trigger big fish to take. This is when the largest predator fish come out to hunt because they can easily ambush a big meal below the surface.

The best way to present a mouse pattern is to dead drift or wake it on the water's sur-

face. You can watch the movement of the drifting fly and wait for the interrupting rise of a large trout. Not only is it exciting to wonder what is lurking below the glare, these hours might be the only time to fool big trout that receive a lot of pressure.

This tactic is similar to timing the wind blowing hoppers off the bank or the hay or grass being cut along the stream's edge, triggering a hopper hatch. Swollen rivers that are flooded to the bank can sweep mice into the river from the edges that are normally exposed. When the season produces higher flows than ever, you want to dead drift the high-water banks on the river's edge with a mouse. Remember that during this time a lot of the mice will drown, making a drag-free presentation the best.

When selecting the right mouse imitation for the job, look for patterns that have a flat belly to ride low on the water's surface as well as enough foam or hair to prevent the fly from sinking.

TIMING PRIME TEMPERATURE

Problem: I can't figure out the optimal river temperature for active trout.

Solution: Adjust your timing to match prime seasonal and daily temperatures.

It was a memorable moment when client and friend Dave Hoover and I witnessed the warming temperatures drop a ledge of ice the size of a Volkswagen Bug. This image gives new meaning to the term "ice-off."

Temperature can be a big part of correctly timing the trout's period of peak activity, which is the ultimate goal for a good day on the water. Conventional thought about timing can cause problems on the river when many anglers believe the early bird gets the worm. Yes, you will often have less pressure on the river early in the day, but finding open water to fish does not mean the trout will be actively feeding.

First and foremost, never forget to take daily water temperature readings. The best way to learn is by understanding what causes a good day on the river. If you do this on a weekly or monthly basis and keep a journal every year, you will know when the trout's activity will increase or understand why it is not an active day on the river.

Prime water temperature, around 45 degrees or more, starts in the spring. Below this temperature the trout are in a lethargic state; while they will still remain active during the day to feed, it will be slower and produce less results for anglers. Once the water begins to warm, approaching 50 to 55 degrees, the trout will begin to reach their maximum activity temperature, sparking feeding behavior, strong fights, and migration within the waters in which they live. These temperatures will be found into the middle of summer. Once you reach the dog days of summer, you want to start thinking about times during the day when water tempera-

tures are 65 degrees or less. This is often in early morning and late afternoon. The fish in higher temperatures will act sluggish, just like they would in cooler temperatures.

Many variables can affect temperature, from weather to time of day. If the ice is melting slowly in the spring, the temperatures will remain cold until the ice is gone, after which fishing will improve. If a storm rolls in during August, the period before and after the storm will see cooler water and air temperatures, resulting in good trout activity. Lastly, think about the species of fish you are pursuing. For example, rainbow trout prefer cold water that is warming, while brown trout prefer warm water that is cooling. Thus, early morning can be great for rainbows, while afternoon and evening hours can be ideal for browns.

LOW LIGHT = BEST BITE

Problem: I see fish in bright conditions, but they shy away from my flies.

Solution: Make a mental note of where the fish were located and pursue them in low-light conditions the same day, or another day when the weather is bad.

We are all in search of warming weather and bluebird skies for our fishing adventures to remain as comfortable as possible. There are some scenarios that supply the best of both worlds—warm and sunny, with outstanding fishing through the day. What some do not realize is that depending on time of day or weather, you

may have more success in low-light conditions. These scenarios decrease visibility for predators, allowing the trout within the waterways more access to feed and exist free of stress.

In clear water on bright days, you'll often see trout that simply will not feed, or that spook on every cast. This is caused by the

A 7-weight, a full-sink line, a stripping basket, a good location, and the right low-light conditions—all Jeff Lyons needs now on the stillwaters of Nevada's Pyramid Lake is a 20-pounder cruising the drop-off edge.

fish detecting movement from above that looks like a potential predator. For these challenging targets, note what the water looks like. Then that evening or early the following morning return to the areas where you saw big fish earlier. In low light, the same trout that were wary during clear conditions will be more likely to feed when they can no longer detect movement from above. This is often the best time to fish streamers.

The first way to time light is by the hours of a day throughout the year. Usually this consists of early mornings and late afternoons. I match the time of day with the seasons I am fishing for the best results. For example, rainbow, cutthroat, and cuttbow

trout prefer cold water that is warming, making the afternoon bite the most active in the winter and early spring. Brown trout prefer warm water that is cooling, making the early morning, late afternoon, and evening the trout's prime feeding times in late summer and fall. This will give you better options for timing your trout hunts.

Beyond the time of year, weather plays a big role in light levels because it is not based on a timetable and every year it can change. The great thing about timing light from weather is the stormy days are as desirable as the nice sunny days, making you more successful throughout the year. The best example of weather affecting light levels is the black skies of a summer's afternoon rain showers. When the black sky dims the light around you and all you see above is black, the trout, especially brown trout, are fooled into thinking it is nightfall and it is time to feed.

Try to time the correct light as it applies to sight-fishing, not reading the water. I like 45-degree-angled sun in the morning or afternoon. This can supply excellent conditions for viewing into the water when the sun is at your back. Dark skies just before or after a storm can also create an advantage for the angler.

HOPPER TIME

Problem: I am using hoppers with limited success.

Solution: Try timing hopper activity to the influence of weather and man.

Timing is everything when it comes to fishing big food supplies such as hoppers. Yes, you can randomly tie on a big-bodied fly and just try it, but this approach rarely works.

The best way to time a hopper bite is when the food supply is forced off the bank. I wait for heavy wind and, instead of placing the wind at my back for ease of casting, I face it head on. This allows me to present my flies to the bank from which the hoppers are being blown into the water. When matched with a pick-up and lay-down cast, you can cut through 30-mile-an-hour winds. I soon realized after spending time with my good friend Eric Mondragon in Montana that humans

Pat Dorsey holds a great example of why big meals on the surface can result in big rewards. This rainbow could not resist a hopper skating on the surface.

could also cause a hopper feeding frenzy. When farmers or landowners cut the hay or grass in their fields, the big-legged flyers are forced to jump ship and will land on the water's edge, causing the trout to seek their next meal.

The end of a hatch sequence—for example, a "dead time" in complex hatches (from roughly two o'clock to six o'clock in the afternoon)—is an excellent time to switch to a hopper rig. Trout are still used to looking up and may take a bigger attractor in the absence of the hatch. Also, the end of a hatch season, from August to October on many waterways, can produce great hopper conditions.

GO WITH THE FLOW

Problem: The water is fluctuating and the fishing is poor.

Solution: Try changing your approach based on high or low water conditions.

Water flow is one of the best ways to predict when trout are going to be moving into a river from stillwater, beginning to move in the river in which they reside full time, or begin feeding heavily from the food being supplied. The best scenario for the trout is when the water is up or on the rise because it provides cover, oxygen, and food supply. The problem for the angler can be adverse conditions and getting to the water too early or too late when the flows begin to fluctuate.

I get excited when the flows increase, knowing that the change in temperature will get large trout to migrate and supply them with some big food items, increasing my chances at catching some big boys. I look for two things in high water before I even begin my adventure. First, I look for water levels holding at their highest point. This means that the trout that began to move to new

holding and feeding grounds have adjusted to the high-water mark and are holding, waiting for their next meal. Second, I look for when the water has reached its peak and begins to fall. At this point, the water will usually clear up, improving conditions for sight-fishing. The trout continue the same heavy feeding behavior and find a wealth of food. You also stand a better chance in deep-water runs where trout that were dispersing in the higher flows or migrating upriver are now forced into areas with cover.

Low water can also be a friend at its worst point. This drop in flows can result in success at the inlets to stillwaters. This is when large trout that were holding in the river system or in moving water are now forced into the stillwater environment, often with big appetites. Not only is this new territory for them, the confused targets are now in competition for food and will look for any

High and dirty water will produce more food for the trout, and give them cover for protection. Do not hesitate to use big, visible food during this time for great results.

meal. This allows you good chances with numerous disciplines of flies, including drys, nymphs, and streamers. If luck is on your side, there are also times when you are on the water the very minute that flows begin dropping from the high mark. For a few hours large trout will hold where they had cover in big water on the edges even though they are now exposed in the low water.

chapter FOUR

Reading Moving Water

I laugh when I think back to how I learned to read water. It was all thanks to Doug Swisher and his series of fly-fishing videos. I always dreaded the phone call coming from Jim Almond at the Angler's Covey reminding me about my growing number of late days from my VHS rental. Years later he would jokingly remind me that in the end returning the VHS would not matter—it would stop playing halfway through because it had been played and rewound so many times.

I still believe Swisher was one of the best trout instructors in our sport, and his step-by-step approach embedded basics in me that led to success and growth as a full-time guide. He would dissect the river and teach in a simple way that has molded the way that I teach.

For those of you that aren't familiar with Swisher, his approach was excellent. He would initially break down his method on a particular subject into a step-by-step format. He was systematic without being overwhelming. When watching his videos I could retain not only what he was teaching, but also why it was effective and how to use it on my next fishing adventure.

I applied Swisher's approach immediately to guiding. The daily goal of a trip was not to receive a mind-boggling amount of information and then catch a trout. The goal was to take a teaching approach where there was a simple formula for success in hunting trout, not just that day, but any day in the future. Sharing information through instruction makes everyone a better angler.

This applies to reading water. While some guides might explain reading water with a complicated lesson (perhaps a one-hour lecture), other guides might oversimplify it (by fishing the same hole every day). Ultimately, it comes down to three basics: cover, oxygen, and food supply, in that order. If a particular stretch of water provides these three conditions, no matter how known or unknown it may be to other anglers, it is worth fishing—especially the water in between or beyond conventional deeps runs.

CRAYFISH CONFIDENCE

Problem: I am having limited success in deep holding runs using crayfish imitations.

Solution: Try crayfish imitations in the shallows of migration waters. This is where a good number of the rock-dwelling crayfish hold and move.

When we learn the basics of reading water, we begin to learn a thought process that carries on to new water and often into every fly discipline. Deep runs become common areas to look for trout; for the angler using streamers, it is a safety zone that promises large numbers of trout. The problem is anglers getting fixated on targeting and fishing only deep runs, thus passing up some of the best shallow water for delivering crayfish imitations.

Think of the food supplies you are imitating. They all possess different speeds within the water, but most importantly, they live in different environments as well. Crayfish are a huge part of a large trout's diet, and if you start to look for crayfish below the surface, you will soon see a pattern of shallow water and structure where they live. A shallow-water environment one to three feet deep is often the best location to present a crayfish fly like Barr's Meat Whistle. Just like the trout that hold on the edge of a shallow run in wait of a big meal like a hopper, large trout occupy these banks waiting for the chance at a fleeing crayfish that is moving about the river's edge.

I prefer to deliver the flies into the middle of the river and allow them to skitter along the shallow water up to the banks where a lot of the naturals dwell. In deep water it is the reverse; the crayfish hold in the shallow on the edge of the deep run and, if need be, flee to the depths where a large trout is waiting at the drop-off shelf.

If the water you are fishing or where the trout are holding is deep, then rely on the movements of crayfish on the edge of the deep run. I refer to these escaping movements as "stop, drop, and roll." The crayfish swim up and backwards a few feet, and then when they feel safe they will drop to the river bottom. Their bodies mix with the water current, causing them to roll. I mimic this motion with a long 2- or 3-foot strip. An abrupt stop of the strip will mimic the crayfish pause; follow that with another pause, then a twitch to mimic the rolling motion of the natural. This retrieve in shallow water (or if necessary, in deep water) will produce great results for large trout hunting these crawling food supplies.

Find out what type and color of crayfish you are dealing with on a particular waterway either before your trip or by investigating the water in person. Rust or olive? Virile or juvenile? This can make a huge difference, as older crayfish are typically rust-colored with blue claws while their younger counterparts can be olive.

When crayfish move backward in the water to escape predators, their claws stretch straight out in front of their bodies. It is important when you match a suitable imitation that it moves in a streamlined manner.

EYEING EDDIES

Problem: I can't make a proper presentation to that big fish sitting in the eddy.

Solution: Use high-stick and tension-drift line techniques, creating your own drift that follows the food train.

Always keep a low profile when approaching eddies. Trout will often hold in the reverse current close to the river's edge.

Eddies are obvious spots for anglers to look for trout. However, you simply cannot get a proper drift in an eddy when using a conventional drift, or mend, that you would use when fishing in the main river channel. An eddy's drag is so intense that your flies will be immediately pulled out of the trout's feeding lane.

I am a huge fan of presenting just the leader with high-stick and tension in the swirling water. This lets you keep in line with the flies at all times by having your rod tip above your rig, preventing drag. At the same time you can lift or drop your rod tip to control depth and determine if the fish are high or low in the water column. If it is simply impossible to get close to the eddy to present your flies, or the eddy is too big, try mending downstream or leading the flies with a shoot mend in front of your indicator or rig. By repeating this motion with the mends, you are now matching the current speed your flies are being directed, making for less drag and more positive presentations in the awkward currents.

Before even attempting to fish the eddy, make sure you are aware of which direction the fish are holding. Sometimes they are facing downstream in a counterclockwise current, while other times they are facing the main flow before it starts to backflow into the eddy. Make sure you are delivering the fly head-on to the fish and not to their backs.

HIGH AND DRY

Problem: It looks like the trout have stopped rising amid the high noon sun.

Solution: Try finding dark water where trout can still rise in the shade.

High walls like the ones seen here in Cheesman Canyon supply great shade for the trout to rise, even at high noon.

At high noon on a sunny day, it's common to see trout that are exposed in open water retreating to the depths to find cover from predators. While you can switch to subsurface flies in pursuit of feeding fish, you will then pass up a chance at midday and afternoon hatches that can trigger some of the largest trout to feed.

Instead of starting in the standard calm water, begin your search for rising trout along the river's edge and structure in dark waters. Shadows cast on the edge of the water or on the sides of structure are the best locations for large trout to feed without the threat of being seen from above. From 10 o'clock in the morning through the afternoon, I hunt for shadows, and I often target them first for rising trout. Take time to investigate any dark water, knowing the water will be harder to see than in the bright conditions.

If you are having difficulty seeing into the shadows during high and sunny conditions, you can also pause and listen for the trout rising. This is especially true for browns with a bigger kype and jaw; they make a sucking sound when they come to the surface to consume a meal. Listening can lead you to an area where the bubbles or riseforms come into view.

REACTING TO THE RISE

Problem: I matched a caddis imitation to the splash riseforms on the water with no success.

Solution: Take the time to investigate the insect and the trout to determine the insect's movement.

When dealing with rising trout, it is common for anglers to connect a specific riseform to a certain insect. For example, a splash rise during caddis season means the trout are eating on the surface. This can be true, but most of the time trout are also reacting to the movements they see from below.

When you fish dry flies, the first and most important thing to do is watch the insects and the trout's reaction before you determine the best approach. We all know the conventional methods for trout rising to specific insects, such as a splash as a trout consumes an escaping caddis, or a gentle sip as a spinner moves by. You may think that trout rise a certain way for certain insects, but I have noticed trout performing several different riseforms to consume the same natural food source on the water's surface. This includes trout tipping and sipping to consume a hopper blown off the river's edge, or making an aggressive splash as they rise to consume a spinner in a fast-moving riffled run. At first this was a surprise, but then I started to understand that the trout were simply responding to the insect's behavior. The same insect behaves in different ways, depending on the conditions. To adjust how you present the fly, take a step back and watch an adult drifting downstream. Then watch the reaction from the trout when it takes the food source. If the fly is moving or fluttering on the surface when the fish takes, you know that imparting that same movement to your fly will result in more takes. If the fish are feeding with sipping rises, don't skitter your fly.

Water speed also affects the way in which trout rise. For example, if a trout is holding in front of a rock where breaking water speeds up around the structure, any adult insect that drifts by is going to speed up with the current. In this situation, even stationary insects look like they are escaping. This "escaping" food might trigger the type of aggressive rise that would come from a trout chasing skittering caddis or other active insects.

To simplify your approach, try to imagine what the trout sees as it is looking up at the water's surface while the silhouette of an insect drifts by. This will help you have a better understanding of how a fish will rise to consume its meal. If the water is slick or slow moving, the silhouette of the fly will stay in the same place. The trout will consume its food slowly because the food does not appear to be escaping. If the water in

which the trout is holding is moving fast, the trout's reaction will be more aggressive to ensure that its meal will not escape. This also applies to trout that are willing to move numerous feet across or within a run into different current speeds. For example, you may be casting to a large brown in a calm eddy when suddenly the fish sees a food source drifting downstream in a faster current in the middle of the river, then decides to hold there. You could apply movement to your drift because the fish is now holding in a fast run where the natural insects would also display the same movements.

Take the time to identify the water the trout is feeding in and the trout's reaction. Observation is key when you are dealing with unusual water flows, places where slow and fast water meet, or where water breaks around structures or objects in the river.

By nature, trout in rivers are relatively lazy when it comes to consuming their food. They hold in feeding lanes, waiting for the food to come to them. They will aggressively pursue a meal as long as they are replenishing the nutrients that were lost in catching the meal. In Alaska, one of the best topwater patterns is a mouse, because a hungry trout cannot pass up the protein supply of such a large source of food. Sometimes fish will abandon cover and oxygen requirements if there is an abundance of food. Use this to your advantage.

BEYOND CONVENTION

Problem: My conventional methods are not working.

Solution: Try thinking outside the box, or adapting a common technique.

Avoid getting stuck in a routine and try searching in unconventional places for trout. ROSS PURNELL

nglers often get stuck in a groove where they look for the same things, or they rig the same way and don't challenge new areas or consider new ideas. I found myself doing this for a few years with reading water. I always relied on the cover, oxygen, and food supply to lead me to areas that hold trout, such as drop-offs at the head of a run, eddies, tailouts, and holes around structure. While these areas still held fish, I started finding fewer fish and more wary trout. I then began exploring beyond these conventional areas and found other ways to read water beyond my normal criteria.

With pressure increasing every year, trout are now so stressed from anglers moving above that they are changing where they hold and feed. What used to be a shelter lie has now become a feeding lie. I call these locations the "waters in between." Shallow, more turbulent areas between deep runs have less pressure and provide an environment where large trout can feed. If you take the time to inspect these areas, you will soon realize there is more water to explore here than where you were fishing before. When you're comfortable targeting these in-between waterways, you will be covering the entire section of water you fish, not just the best spots of the past.

When hunting the waters in between deep runs, look for structure, as deep drop-offs may not exist. Structure can be rocks, boulders, or logjams. Try judging depth by color change, as depressions as small as two feet by three feet can hold large trout.

With less depth and dark waters to contrast against the trout's body, you want to concentrate on locating parts of the trout's body when you search these swift waterways. Some of my favorites are the white of the fish's mouth, tails, and pectoral fins.

READING MIGRATION

Problem: I don't know what water to hunt during the migration.

Solution: Find the path that the fish are traveling in based on depth and water speed.

any believe that a river will hold plentiful numbers of large trout in the spring and fall and that if you fish every day you'll have a shot at a giant. Yes, there will always be a chance to hook a big fish during the right time of year, but guessing and then simply covering water can be a waste of time.

If I am standing on the river's edge looking downstream, I search for pathways where trout can move. I try to think like a moving trout by locating deep seams, riffled runs with disturbances on the surface providing cover, breaks in flow created by structure, or the deepest flow entering a run. When you put all these sections together, you see a giant snaking seam that flows downriver. It's similar to sketching a pencil path on a paper maze. Most of the time this is the pathway that fish will follow when they migrate and stage during a run. I use this path to determine where I fish. For example, some sections of a river look ideal for holding trout, but the water leading into or out of these sections is so shallow that large trout cannot move without being detected. I avoid these areas and look for water that supplies more depth and cover.

I also rely on structure more than deep runs. Even if the water around a rock is shallow, the water on the river bottom below will wash out over time and provide a structure pocket where the trout can hold. These undercuts are some of the best areas to find large trout. I make a point to fish or investigate every structure point I come across in a day—not the deepest runs—because I have investigated the pathways.

Think about the stopping points that trout need when they move. If you see a long, riffled run leading into a deep pool, or a section that is littered with rocks, always stop to hunt these areas. Trout will hold and rest here before they continue their journey upriver.

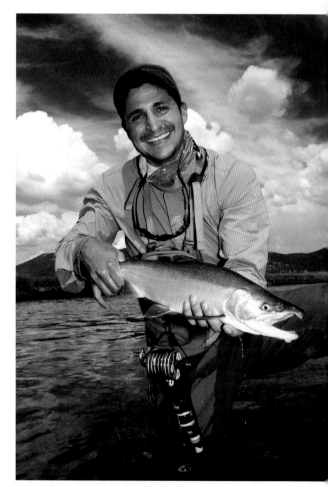

Always think early when you time a fish migration. This is when the trout and salmon are fresh and full of energy for a memorable fight.

RIFFLED REWARDS

Problem: All of the conventional runs are occupied by other anglers, and I don't know where to start.

Solution: Dissect the fast riffled water between the deep runs. These areas are ideal protection zones for trout.

Riffles are prime feeding zones for trout, offering cover, oxygen, and food. These anglers are positioned at the edge of a classic riffled run on the Bitterroot River in Montana.

When we are taught to "read" the water, prime spots to look for trout include pools and deep runs; however, on pressured public water, trout often prefer riffles. Riffles not only have broken water which obscures a trout's view of you but they are also food factories. In addition, riffles also produces oxygen that keeps the trout healthy, especially in warm water conditions. For these reasons, riffles are the best feeding grounds for trout.

Riffled waters are prime locations for sight-fishing because the image the trout see above the water's surface is distorted by the rolling waves of water. This will allow you to get closer to large trout, permitting you to see the take and understand how trout move when they feed. This knowledge can be applied to many situations: a fish looking for midges in warmer, shallow waters in winter; a trout looking for drowned spinners during a dense summer hatch; or a big predatory fish looking for a large topwater meal blown onto the surface from the river's edge. These riffled rewards found in the water between conventional runs will improve your results and reveal new details about the waters you've fished since you started fly fishing.

Keep in mind that most of the time the water will be shallow, making it tough to get the long drifts you might be accustomed to in deeper water. Systematically fan the run by making a grid and presenting flies a short distance in each drift—10 feet or so. This will prevent you from snagging river bottom and produce more swings at the end of the drift, which mimics an emerging meal and keeps your flies taut above the river bottom where suspended trout are feeding.

Lastly, keep depth control in mind. Unlike in deep runs or shelves where you want flies to sink quickly, here you want the flies to sink at a slow pace so they remain in the middle column of the water, often 12 to 24 inches below the surface. Micro shots or small pinches of putty will start you off light. Another way to control depth is by removing unnatural weight and relying on plastic beads; you will get a slow sink rate and achieve long drifts to shallow feeding trout without snagging the river bottom as you would with heavy metal beads.

SOFTWATER BREAKS

Problem: The flow is too high to read seams and drop-offs, so I don't know where to fish.

Solution: Try targeting softwater breaks, areas that trout can hold without fighting the river's current.

Every fly fisher will experience high flows and the challenge of finding water that trout can hold in without expending too much of their energy. Large trout especially are lazy and are not willing to fight the current. The problem in high flows is that you can't see structure and seams that are visible at normal flows, making it hard to read the water and hard to locate proper holding spots for the trout.

When water covers structure and a heavy current washes out seams, you can still fish these locations, even in dirty water. You want to target softwater breaks that are visible on the water's surface. They can be calm windows of water in heavy currents, a slow sec-

Pat Dorsey hunts a stretch of soft water away from the main channel on the San Juan River in late winter.

tion in the middle of a fast current, or points on the river's edge that extend out from the bank like little peninsulas. Slower water speeds allow the trout to take a break from the heavy current. Lastly, islands are an angler's best friend in high-flow conditions. Small side channels that in other seasons normally look like a trickle can hold trout escaping the river's heavy current. Large trout avoiding the flood can be found from the entrance of the side channel to the river's main current.

Many times the merging seams around islands are the slowest sections of a racing water way. It is common to find large trout here, and they can be in plentiful numbers. Your drifts will not always be long, and the trick is getting down to the fish in short distances. Thinking ahead one split shot, or pinch of putty, add more weight to achieve the proper depth. It's a safe bet in these high water marks you'll need more lead to reach the fish than in calm water.

SWEARING BY STRUCTURE

Problem: I can't get a proper drift around structure without snagging and losing flies.

Solution: Try "threading the needle" by drifting in the seams in between the structure.

Rarely will you meet a large brown that is not holding in or near structure. These giants are aggressive hunters that rely on objects for protection and for ambushing prey.

The problem anglers can have in locating large trout is that they look in areas where it seems impossible to get a drift. Structure is a prime example. Yes, there are going to be locations around structure in which trout cannot be reached, but there are areas where they can be caught. You will see more giant fish in these areas than in conventional waters. I also believe anglers shy away from structure because you lose the length in most of your drifts or presentations. Long lines lead many anglers to believe the more line you have out, the better chance you have of catching a fish. The shadow-casting scene in *A River Runs Through It* did nothing to dispel this notion! But contrary to popular thought, you don't have to think long all the time.

There are many forms of structure. Rocks, logs, vegetation, docks—the list is endless. The most common structure we see in waters throughout the world are stones and rocks, both naturally occurring and planted by man. This is a safe place for large fish. Even if the rock is only a foot in circumference, it is still a magnet for trout because they feel safer around it. Just as I do with runs of moving water, I inspect the structure areas and try to deliver flies in, around, and through every inch of these "stone zones." I have found more trout breaking 30 inches in these locations than in any other type of water. You need line tension when presenting

to structure. Don't use a drag-free drift that cannot be lifted, dropped, or pulled through the water around the structure. This will let you drift without snagging in little seams— and avoiding snags is the key to getting the flies to the fish.

Don't forget to fish in front of the rock as well as behind it. Many anglers believe from literature and movies that trout hold predominantly *behind* rocks in the river. My experience has been the opposite. Some of the largest fish in any river place themselves in front of the rock because a large washout section forms at this location and they don't have as much of a fight with the water's current. While fish do hold behind rocks, remember that they will always pick the area where they can consume a meal while expending the least energy in doing so.

VEGETATION VALLEYS

Problem: There is too much vegetation to achieve a proper drift.

Solution: Find open-water valleys where you can drift your flies without snags.

As the summer sun penetrates the water, vegetation may cover up your favorite fishing locations, or grass will continue to grow, making it impossible to achieve the same drift or presentation as when the waterways were open. Problems result when anglers begin to move and search for open water without first examining the water where they know trout prefer to hold.

This vegetation is a relief for large trout that have been exposed in runs. It allows them to feed without stress or worry, and it gives anglers a chance to hook up with more large trout. You can often find pockets in the vegetation, but long strips of open-water "valleys" can be found in almost all of this green structure.

Jay Nichols cautiously scans the clear water valleys in between grass-choked runs on Big Spring Creek in Pennsylvania. Even seeing a tail sliding out below the vegetation is enough to make a stealth presentation worthwhile knowing a fish is there.

Even if the valley of open water is only six inches wide, it will allow you to get a long drift and achieve depth at the same time. Ideal structure allows you to wade up to the edge of the open water; the steep vegetation walls prevent the fish from seeing side to side. You can present to some of the largest brown trout of the year and be only a few feet away—and in the cover of vegetation, you can still see your target in detail.

To present effectively in these situations, use tension during your drift with the rod tip directly above the flies and leading your rig downstream at a 45-degree angle. One of my favorite techniques is "tension drifting." It allows you full control of your flies and is easy to adjust if needed. By simply lifting or dropping the rod tip, you can control your depth or, by leading or stopping the rod tip from moving downstream, you can control the speed with which your flies move. This will let you fit into these valleys whether they are big or small, deep or shallow. In addition to tension drifting, twitching your flies can also be very effective. In some situations having the rod tip low and close to the water's surface will spook fewer trout. From this rod position, if you twitch the tip 6 to 12 inches, the flies will lift in the water column, preventing snags. I will often twitch the flies into position up stream of the trout where I can then pause the rod and allow the flies to drift accurately into the trout's viewing lane.

TARGETING MIGRATION WATERS

Problem: I can't find the large trout during migration.

Solution: Try looking for staging runs, or holding grounds close to the stillwater.

When hunting large migratory trout, anglers can get stuck believing the best waters to target are classic runs with drop lines and seams. Yes, these waters are great areas for trout to find cover, and they are the areas where most anglers fish. The problem is finding trout that are willing to feed.

I break down the water into three sections that hold trout during the different moving stages of the migration. The first are staging runs, typically runs that possess cover for the trout from water color and depth, allowing the trout a chance to stage before the spawning season arrives. Some of my favorite spots to fish in staging waters are deep runs close to the stillwater the river flows into. By fishing these areas, you will intercept the trout before other anglers can catch them, resulting in more hookups. I find the best staging runs are deep and off-color and possess one or more types of structure on the river bottom.

The second sections are rest runs. These are often calm, deep runs in which trout can rest before continuing to migrate. Such spots are often found in or near fast runs in which the fish must expend energy. To locate trout in resting areas, look for runs that are calm but not so deep that you lose visibility. Remember that the fish are only resting; they are readying to move from this location later in the day.

The last sections are migrating runs or fast seams and riffles that see moving fish heading to calm waters for refuge. Some trout blast through this water while others take a slow approach. When locating fish in these turbulent waters, wait for the trout to stop—even briefly—before you make a cast. Moving trout with migration on the mind are not as willing to feed.

Once you locate prime migration waters, target the low-light hours of the day when large trout are known to hunt their prey. John Barr hunts the Yampa River near nightfall.

chapter FIVE

Stillwater Success

My earliest memories of fishing stillwaters are from growing up in Colorado Springs, where I had a pond in a park only a two-minute-walk from my house. I spent many afternoons and weekends catching bluegill, crappie, and largemouth bass. What I didn't realize then, but know now, is that those adventures would give me the confidence to fish stillwaters and learn fundamentals such as targeting, structure points, drop-off zones, depth control, and which flies would get the attention of cruising fish.

I now use these skills to pursue some of the country's largest trout. I believe one of the best ways to make yourself a complete angler is to understand the difference between fish that hold still in moving water and fish that move in stillwaters.

It was November 2012 and I was on the hunt for Great Lakes browns with friend and fellow angler Phil Tereyla. The trip was timed to capitalize on the high flows that cause large browns to migrate up swollen tributaries. Unfortunately, Mother Nature threw us a

curveball. The water that was supposed to be high and dirty had dropped to the lowest flow I have ever seen: a measly 7 cubic feet per second (cfs), which I believe qualifies as a trickle. Yes, we were disappointed, but we kept positive and decided to hunt the edges of the harbors and bays in an effort to come home with some sort of fish tale. In our determination, we didn't sleep for two days, and we fished eighteen-hour stretches on foot, kicking around bays in Outcast Prowlers during the evening. We did, of course, take breaks to become Home Depot's most knowledgeable individuals on which spotlight emits the most lumens.

Soon, we knew we'd made the right call. The edge of the lake was teeming with big cruising alligator look-alikes that were forced down from the lack of river water, looking to feed before ice took the lake for the season. Day and night, we made short presentations of only 20 feet or less; I assure you that fighting trout while battling sleep deprivation makes for a memorable experience. I felt like I was trying to hold the rod and reel with my elbows. Finally, we accomplished our goal that I have replayed in my mind many times since: two browns over twenty pounds.

In this chapter we'll take a closer look at the stillwater techniques that land fish and unlock the door to new areas for anglers to hunt.

Hidden at the base of giant granite walls, Box Lake in Rocky Mountain National Park was a welcome sight after an extreme hike off the beaten path.

LOCATING TROUT IN STILLWATERS

Problem: I cannot locate trout in different stillwaters.

Solution: Try looking for three ingredients: drop-offs, structure, and vegetation.

Often, the inlet to a stillwater will hold some of the largest trout. The constant flow of fresh, migratory waterways will funnel big fish in on the Great Lakes. Here an angler hunts brown trout from a rocky point.

Fishing stillwaters can be an intimidating experience because the water is wide and open, making locating the fish tough. Yes, you can start by finding deep water that drops from the shallow edge, but the trout require other areas and structure to survive.

The three key ingredients to stillwater success are structure (primarily that along the water's edge), drop-off points and ledges with a severe change in depth, and vegetation in deeper portions of the water. In spring trout cruise the water's edge in search of food as the ice melts away, but more important is the heat this water near the edge provides. Even when the fish cruise like river trout, they still need cover to feel safe. If the edge you are fishing has a flat sand bottom with no cover, the fish will be wary and not want to feed. Drop-offs also supply cover for important trout meals like crayfish, mayfly nymphs, and midges. You can locate these drop-offs by looking for a distinct color change in the water, often to dark blue or green.

As the water warms and sunlight bakes the surface, trout will disperse all over the stillwater, and vegetation will grow like skyscrapers. These towering veg clumps are the key to locating trout in the depths of a fishery. The open water in between is where trout cruise and feed. Kick out or drive in by boat to see open pathways where you can hang your nymphs or retrieve your streamers without snags and get to feeding trout. Remember that trout in stillwaters are always looking for their next meal, so don't get stuck in one area. Try to land your fly or flies as close as possible to the edge of the weeds, knowing that a giant could be holding in the vegetation, waiting to attack a moving meal.

GET TO THE POINT

Problem: I keep spooking trout in the reservoir while looking for new locations to fish.

Solution: Try positioning yourself along points to intercept the cruising trout.

Preventing trout from detecting you in stillwaters sometimes feels impossible. Whether it's the movement of the rod, or the disturbance of your line as it lands on the water surface, these cruising trout are difficult to fool. Anglers must recognize that the trout are always moving to seek food.

Before anything, look where you'll fish to see the target and its behavior. In stillwaters this will tell you in which direction (clockwise or counterclockwise) and how deep the trout is cruising. During ice-off and on high mountain lakes is where I encounter most sight-fishing for trout. These are also some of the best times for targeting larger fish.

Once you see the trout's traveling lane, you want to find a position on the water's edge that provides a viewing lane at a 45-degree angle left or right. At this angle you can see the fish coming from a distance, not when it's directly in front of you. The most common viewing lanes I find on the edge are from angled sunlight—the coloration cast on the water's surface from structures along the stillwater's edge, such as trees or cliffs. Once you see the traveling trout in the viewing lane, you want to present your fly just past the distance you think the fish are cruising off the bank. By casting past the trout, you set up a presentation that will intercept the

If you concentrate on points and peninsulas on the stillwater's edge you will intercept cruising trout. These edge positions will put you closer to the middle drop-off zones. JAY NICHOLS

traveling fish. Once you spot your target, you can strip in some line to be right in trout's path. This often provokes a reaction from the trout and causes them to look at or take the fly. By having the line and flies in place, you are also eliminating any chance of movement above the trout that can spook the fish.

PATIENCE FOR STILLWATER BASS

Problem: My typical trout retrieve doesn't work for bass.

Solution: Try a long pause after the drop. Bass are known to suction up food from the bottom of waterways.

You can find success fishing for bass with imitations like baitfish, crayfish, worms, and poppers. The takes are exciting, but when using these imitations many anglers use too much action and speed on the retrieve. While bass are reaction-based feeders, they are also known to suck the food in with their large bucket mouth. The best and easiest way for them to do this is by searching the edges or bottom of stillwaters.

I remember the first time I encountered big bass using a slow retrieve. I was in Houston, Texas, with my good friend John Barr. John taught me to use his design, a Meat Whistle, by using a slow hand-over-hand retrieve, or a lift-and-drop retrieve at a slow pace—so slow you are sometimes looking for the line to barely move to the side just above the surface to set. Having this much patience for bass can be tough, but the reward can be big bucketmouth action. When you are bass fishing, most of your takes are during the drop, not when the fly is lifting. This may be because a food source that is dropping looks injured, as bass takes are aggressive and opportunistic. During a long pause, the Whistle simply sits on the bottom pulsating and undulating, driving bass crazy and triggering the Dyson vacuum effect from the bass on your fly.

SAND PUFFS FOR CARP

Problem: The carp are feeding close to the edge and are hard to reach undetected.

Solution: Cast ahead into their "feeding highway" and move the fly when it is in the carp's view creating a puff of sand.

The best way to approach carp is from a low position on the stillwater's edge, or a platfrom on a boat, using long leaders to avoid being seen. Even with such a cautious approach, anglers still must get a cast to these fish without the leader and fly landing on the surface too close to the target.

Instead of directly approaching the carp, watch and determine the path where they feed as they move along the bottom. Sometimes they move along the edge without stopping, while other times they cruise in circles as they feed. Once you determine the feeding highway, wait for the fish to move out of casting view and find a marker on the reservoir bottom, such as a rock or patch of weeds; this will become your target for casting and presenting the fly.

Don't follow the fish as they move. Instead, cast your fly and let it rest on the bottom near your target. Then wait for the fish to return to that area. Once the carp are within a few feet, perform a small strip of about 6–12 inches, enough to cause a puff of sand to stir up the bottom where your fly was resting. This will cause the fish to investigate—and often feed. Crayfish in their natural stillwater environment will crawl along, and when they are spooked, flee by flipping their tails and lifting up while they swim backward. This creates the same puff of sand as your fly does, and this sand is one

When carp are happy, they feed slowly. Lead the fish, or school of fish, with your fly settled on the bottom. With a simple strip, you will stir up a puff of sand, alerting the carp that a meal is below.

of the key things feeding carp look for while on the hunt.

Many anglers prefer to fish for carp in clear water because they can see the targets cruising. Off-color water, however, can pro-vide added cover for both the carp and the angler, making the sand puff even more important. This sand is different from the nor-mal "smoke" moving around in the water.

SLIP INDICATORS

Problem: I need a long leader to reach the trout, but I keep losing fish by not having enough reach to get them in the net.

Solution: Use indicators that slip down to the first fly after the hook lift.

Some stillwater anglers struggle to achieve a controlled depth of up to 20 feet with a long leader that, when placed below an indicator, does not cause problems when netting a fish. When you're sitting waist deep in the water or kneeling over the edge of a boat, however, even a long-handled net can't provide enough reach to net the trout on such a long leader.

To solve this problem, use a slip indicator that releases the wedge loop on the indicator when you set the hook on a fish, causing the indicator to slide down to the first fly. This allows you to net trout effectively, even with a 20-foot leader. With the main indicator body slid onto the leader before the flies are attached, the hole in the middle will let you determine how far up you need to slide the indicator. Use a quarter-inch loop at the top of the indicator and slide the plastic insert with half the loop into the circular hole. This will keep the indicator in place for fishing but allow it to slip free on the set.

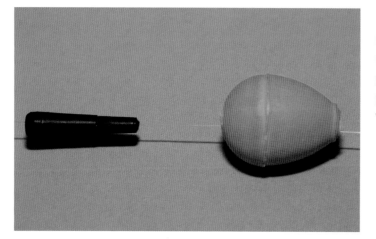

1. Insert the nonrigged leader and tippet into the hollow slip indicator and the plastic insert. Slide both pieces up to the depth you want to present at.

2. To peg the indicator in place, grab the indicator with the thumb and index finger of your dominant hand. Use your middle, ring, and pinky fingers to grip the leader below so it does not slide when inserting the plastic peg. Mimic the same grip with your opposite hand. With the leader below the indicator and above the plastic peg that is firmly in place, slowly insert the plastic peg. This will cause the leader in between to form a loop. Leave the peg loose once you've inserted it.

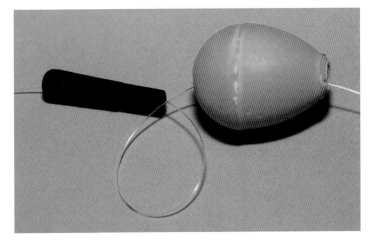

3. Adjust the loop lying next to the plastic insert by pulling down on the leader. You do not want the loop to go beyond the top of the plastic insert. Push the insert into the indicator to place the leader. Use force but not so much that the loop cannot move when pressure is applied. This will allow you to cast without the indicator slipping; just remember to leave it loose enough that it will slip when you set the hook.

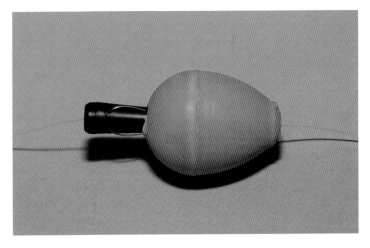

THE PIKE HINGE

Problem: The pike are following the fly to my feet without a take.

Solution: Try a 90-degree hinge in the line to change direction of the fly.

I have always enjoyed the challenge of fishing new water and targeting new species of fish. I believe the knowledge you gain from one target can lead to new ideas for another. Trout are selective creatures but pike, in my opinion, are even more selective and will learn to recognize fly patterns, or pressure quickly. When these "water wolves" become wary, it is common for pike to follow the oversize fly right to your feet. Making a last-ditch effort to move your rod in a figure eight position around your boat or where you are standing might work, but it is almost impossible to get a proper hook set and maintain control of the fly's movement when all the line is in past the first guide.

Pike, muskie, and tiger muskie have a partial blind spot in the front of their jaw. Because their eyes are positioned on the sides of their head in an upright position, they can lose sight of a meal when it is right in front of them. I believe they can still sense the fly movement and they will continue the chase. At the last minute, they will abruptly take the fly as it reappears in the viewing lane when the fly is swept hard to the side.

Knowing how important this sudden change in the direction of the fly was, I started throwing a huge mend (hinge) in my line after I made an accurate cast. This allowed me to retrieve my flies normally in the first part of my presentation. Then, without my having to adjust anything, the flies would turn around 90 degrees following the path of the hinge in my line—causing any fish in pursuit to attack! Don't worry about casting a long mend to achieve distance. Keep the mend around ten feet from boat, or where you wade. This will give you close distance to set and not miss the pike's grab.

The first thing you will learn hunting toothy critters is how these water wolves follow your fly to your kneecaps on the stillwater or river's edge. Changing direction of the fly will usually trigger a take when the fish thinks its meal will escape. JAY NICHOLS

CALM-WATER PRESENTATIONS

Problem: The water is too calm, so the trout are not feeding without cover.

Solution: Try making small fly-moving strips to get a reaction take.

You don't often see calm conditions on large bodies of water, such as here on Alaska's Lake Iliamna. Think deep water to locate fish when there is no cover on the surface.

In stillwaters, a slight chop on the surface not only helps move your flies but also provides some overhead cover, and sense of protection, for trout. Trout in stillwaters constantly move in search of food. That means you want to get their attention when they swim by your imitations. When conditions are calm, wait until your flies have sunk to the proper depth and then apply a small strip every fifteen to thirty seconds until it is time to recast. This will cause your flies to jig up and down below the surface or skate across the surface.

Unlike many river scenarios, you can also move your flies effectively while keeping control of your line with a mend. Instead of mending while your indicator or dry fly remains still, slightly overpower the mending motion. This will also cause your flies to jig or skate.

Since fish typically strike when your flies are moving and the calm water is forcing you to mimic movement, try adding that needed movement to your flies by mending, not stripping. This provides more slack and prevents you from putting too much tension on your line, which could cause a fish to break off.

Lastly, if the targets become too selective, try removing the indicator and fish your imitation with a slow retrieve. The reward for using nymphs in this situation is less disturbance on the water's surface after each cast, and it matches the insects' and crustaceans' movements below the water's surface.

STILLWATER STARTING POINTS

Problem: This water is so vast and apparently featureless that I feel lost and don't know where to start fishing.

Solution: Try a three step approach on all stillwaters.

I believe many do not explore stillwaters because they are more comfortable reading moving water to find trout. This is a mistake because fly fishers who ignore stillwaters are missing their shot at large trout that do not receive much pressure. While conditions are different from river settings, you can dissect a stillwater quickly, regardless of size, and locate its trout. In my youth, I often felt lost when gazing at the surface of so many big stillwaters. I soon realized that the best way to break down any fishery is to simplify your approach. For stillwaters I use three starting points to locate the best water for my next adventure.

Take yourself back to the school playground when you climbed on top of monkey bars to call out "I'm king of the mountain." The goal is the same when scouting stillwaters: you want to walk, park, or climb to the highest point of any stillwater to see the lay

of the land and develop a plan of where to fish. A great example of using height to your advantage is the stairsteps on Pyramid Lake near Reno, Nevada. Anglers use three- to six-foot ladders to spot trout cruising or to see drop lines. In the bays of the Great Lakes, breaker walls give you a vertical view of the large trout the waters hold. In the high country of Rocky Mountain National Park, the descent from the many nearby hills gives you a clear view of the stillwater nestled in a bowl. Conversely, this high point could simply be the highest parking lot you can find aside any public stillwater.

The second step is finding points to intercept trout while they cruise. In many stillwaters there are islands or peninsulas that extend out toward the middle of the water. These points are an effective way to present to trout toward the middle of the lake, pond, or reservoir, and ensure a drop line that you

The first things I look for on any stillwater are color changes or drop-off points. This great example is on Nevada's Pyramid Lake.

can cast toward from a boat. The point can be big or small in size. If the point has structure on it or descends from a cliff or wall, it can also become a great spot for relief from wind and weather, making for great fishing throughout the day.

Color change is the final ingredient for locating valuable stillwater. Any time you see a color change from shades like light green to aqua green to navy blue, you know there are three depth levels that will hold trout.

Weather also affects the color of the water. When wind stirs the edges of a stillwater with chopping waves, the water will turn the color of the bank's soil and bleed out from the edge, creating huge mud lines that provide cover for trout. Remember to fish in the dirty water, not just the clear-water transition on the edge. With full protection from above, the trout feel safe enough to feed as close as a few feet from shore.

BIG-FISH CHOP

Problem: The lack of wind is supplying less cover for the trout to feed and minimal movement to my flies with the lack of waves.

Solution: Look for days that supply winds of 10 to 20 mph. Known for harsh weather, spring will offer many hours of big-fish chop.

Wind is your friend on any stillwater. It supplies a great jigging action for your flies below, triggering cruising trout under the cover of the moving surface to feed.

For most anglers, the spring will deliver wind that is unwelcome, but the stillwater angler has a happy term for the breeze: Big-Fish Chop. Disturbance on a stillwater's surface supplies trout with cover, and the rolling chop creates waves that add a constant jigging movement to your flies, in addition to helping melt any ice. If you are using nymph rigs, this movement can trigger more takes from cruising trout.

During the spring, most of the absorbed heat is on the surface of the stillwater. The wind blows this warmer water into various points, bays, and shallows, creating the perfect feeding temperatures of around 50 degrees. Following the warm water is vegetation, sediment, and most important, food blown into the shallows. This creates scum lines that expand farther out from shore as the wind blows the water toward the edge. In heavy winds, concentrate on these food banks and target the clear water just past the change line. Fish school up in large numbers while searching through the muck for food.

The ideal chop is around one- to six-inch riffles on the surface. This imparts just enough vertical motion to add movement to your flies and provide proper cover for the trout. When your chop turns to waves rolling on the surface, you'll need to add more weight and length to your rig to adjust for the lift because your flies will begin to move drastically up and down. Whether they are subtle or intense, these wind conditions are the key to fishing on stillwaters.

Additionally, try different angles when fishing into the wind. When the gusts are head on, your flies will be pushed back directly to you with less drag in the water. This will achieve more depth. If the wind is blowing in from the side, you will have more tension when your flies ride in the water. Try both to determine the action the trout prefer in the windy environment.

Even a little chop of 3 to 6 inches is enough to trigger movement in your rig and a response from cruising trout.

Seeing is Believing

After my third year of guiding and teaching anglers the fundamentals of fly fishing, I began to suspect there was more to fishing than just adapting to the river conditions and leaving everything else to chance. Until then I had been teaching my clients how to cast, present a drag-free drift, and watch the indicator to know when to set. While this worked, I felt that my clients and I should spend more time hunting for a visual of our target and that blindly fishing into a run was not the most efficient way to fish.

I began to walk the river for a couple of hours before meeting my clients. I looked for potential targets, and then took my clients to the same areas where I had seen fish so that we could try to locate them again under different light conditions. This was my breakthrough; "seeing is believing" became my fishing motto, and I realized that sight-fishing was so much more than finding a fish rising on the surface.

My best demonstration of the power of sight-fishing occurred in the fall of 2006 in upstate New York while I was on an adventure with my good friends John Barr and Frank Martin. While most people think of sight-fishing as a tool for use in clear water, I learned on this trip that sighting fish is possible even in high and dirty water.

We were filming *Landing the Trout of Your Life*. We had timed our trip to coincide with the first heavy rains of the fall. During this time, large browns move into the swelling creeks to feed on chinook eggs. While we were there, a five-day nor'easter dropped so much rain that the creeks grew to an almost unmanageable size. Great Lakes brown trout have distinct black tails and bellies, and I had to adjust my sights to spot these markings on the edges of the banks as the water started to recede. Had I continued to look for the orange or yellow markings I was used to in Colorado's comparatively clear water, I would not have seen the giants we caught on film.

From that trip, and from many others, I learned that sight-fishing is about seeing parts of a fish, such as a tail—not a detailed view of the entire trout. More often than not, I have landed trout by fishing to a ghostly silhouette or by guessing where the mouth is when I can only see the tail.

This chapter provides valuable information on how to locate trout in dirty water, how to know if they are eating, and how to hunt them effectively in even the most challenging visual conditions. By thinking outside of conventional methods, sight-fishing can become reflexive, and you will use it constantly while fishing.

Notice the distinct coloration on the inside of this large brown trout's mouth. It is common for trout's mouth to turn bright orange or pink in addition to white. Look for these three colors when searching for feeding fish.

A BREAK FROM ROUTINE

Problem: I can't tell the difference between trout and vegetation movement in the water.

Solution: Look for breaks in the object's movements.

When vegetation sways below the water's surface it will repeat the same movement over and over. When trout hold there will be a break at some point in the movement, letting you know the target is a fish.

People commonly ask me, "How do you determine if what you are seeing is a trout and not swaying vegetation on the river bottom?" This problem plagues many fishermen because a trout's body can resemble the shape and movement of vegetation.

If you do not take the time to look for signs that the object is a fish, you will be fooled by vegetation. I look for a break in the motion of the object. Vegetation has a repetitive motion when it moves. In addition to the predictable motion, the end of the vegetation usually does not have a wide base like the fan of a trout's tail would. You should look for a break in the motion when a trout moves side to side or up and down to feed. Fish drift back when they investigate objects below the surface while feeding. To keep your eyes in the same visual area, look below your object of focus and find a marker like a rock on the river bottom. This will let you know if the target has drifted downstream like a trout investigating a meal.

The trout's tail is a big giveaway because it always moves while the fish is holding still. Vegetation will sway or bend from the middle, while a trout's tail is only a few inches long. The tail moves in a confined area.

HUNT ON THE MOVE

Problem: I am hunting trout with a slow approach to see, but the fish I locate are often spooked.

Solution: Use unfocused eyes while hunting water on the move to see the target before it detects you.

I remember seeing anglers moving around the river and trying to sight-fish, their hands cupped around the sides of their faces to create a shadow tunnel. This allowed them to see into the water free of glare from the edges while they were hunched over, holding still and looking in the water. While this is a great way to eliminate glare, cupping your hands eliminates your peripheral vision. Any targets up- or downstream of you can spook, preventing you from seeing the fish at all.

You can create the same effect without losing your peripheral vision, which helps you detect objects out of the corner of your eye. You'll need a wide-brimmed hat, sunglasses, and a buff. My favorite headgear is a Simms eight-panel hat with a wide brim that is dark underneath; the edge of the bill extends down past your glasses on the side of your face. Your sunglasses should be polarized and have thick side shields to prevent any light from penetrating the side of your eyes and distracting your view. Finally, place a dark-colored buff around the back of your hat and wrap it around your face so that it rests below your glasses. This creates a "shadow zone" for your eyes to see out of while all the glare is eliminated from your vision.

Now that you've created a great visual zone, you want to start hunting the water at your walking speed. Keep your eyes focused in front of you looking into a viewing lane with the least amount of glare; then begin to hunt at a moving pace. If the terrain is structure-free, you can move quickly while glancing down periodically to keep your footing. If the terrain is rough, map out step points on the ground before you move forward. This

When you hunt at a normal walking pace you can quickly stop, drop on one knee, and throw to the fish without spooking the target. JAY NICHOLS

allows you to trace your steps so you can be looking into the water while you move. Many people don't realize that you will spook trout when you sight-fish; nonetheless, this still will let you know where the trout was so you can come back later with a stealthy approach.

In some situations you can watch the spooked fish move and relocate to a new feeding or holding area, allowing you another cast. Hunting at your walking speed will let you locate the still and moving targets while you cover ground looking for the next target.

BODY PARTS

Problem: I can't see the trout's body or silhouette when I am hunting in stained water.

Solution: Try looking for body parts that are close to the surface, such as a tail, dorsal fin, pectoral fin, or adipose fin.

Sight-fishing is one of the best ways to become a better angler. It allows you to cover water effectively and learn more about the trout's behavior and movements. The biggest problem is that many anglers look for a detailed image of the trout body, which is visible for only a small percentage of the time.

The first and most important things to look for are the most visible parts of the trout's body; they are closer to the surface and thus easier to detect. I always hunt for the top of the tail or the dorsal fin. Another advantage in locating these body parts, especially the tail, is that they move when the trout holds its position against the current or swims in stillwater.

In dark water or locations with contrasting colors of water, the white of the trout's mouth is a big giveaway to the fish's location and a sign that it is actively feeding. I have found over the years that I sometimes see brighter colors of orange or pink inside the fish's mouth. This is most common in large trout that have a high-protein diet, which changes the pigmentation of a trout's body and the inside of its mouth. Instead of relying on body color to see fish, I look for mouth color of trout that are either feeding or so big that the inside of the lower jaw is exposed even when the trout attempts to close its mouth.

Pectoral fins are another giveaway of holding trout. Because much of the trout's belly color extends down into the pectoral fins, these objects are often exposed. Some of the best times to hunt trout are early and late in the day; these times supply great angled light that will penetrate the translucent fins, giving away the hidden target. Remember

In my home state of Colorado, many of the brook trout have dark backs and red or orange bellies. This native brookie in Pennsylvania was a pleasant surprise in size and color. With a yellow belly and olive back, the only thing that stood out was the lead white stripe on the lower fins. JAY NICHOLS

what glowing colors to look for: orange for brown and cutthroat fins, red for rainbows, and pink with a white lead stripe for a brook trout's fins. This white stripe contrasts well against the river or creek bottom.

HUNTING FOR SHADOWS

Problem: Midday sun has caused the trout to flee from runs where they are exposed.

Solution: Start hunting for shadows of suspended feeding trout that are less wary.

The most exciting part of summer is seeing rising trout as they gorge on an early-morning hatch. This is one of the best sight-fishing experiences any angler can have. But with the good also comes the bad—specifically, at midday when the sun is high overhead and all those trout that were gorging begin to disappear for safety and cover. Many anglers believe that the rush is over when this happens, but in many ways it has just begun.

Sunny conditions can challenge any trout hunter on the water when the fish has a good chance of detecting you in the bright light. One way to avoid spooking trout is by locating fish that have their attention focused on feeding and not movement from above. Shadows the trout cast on the river bottom while suspended in a run are the answer because suspended fish are feeding fish. A great example of this is when sight-fishers look for trout in general, locating silhouettes and movement that are lighter than the river bottom. In the noon sun, search for dark blue or black shadows contrasting against

the river bottom with the trout suspended above.

It's not just the visual that's key. You should also locate a viewing lane that spans out 10 feet or more that will allow you to see the fish from a distance and prevent spooking the fish while it feeds. This is helpful, as you can see the bold color from a greater distance—just look for black. You can give yourself a few more advantages by looking in water with a light bottom that will contrast against the shadow. Riffled runs, sand bars, and tailouts are all good areas known to expose shadows.

Lastly, look for trout shadows next to other shadows. Under sunny skies, trout are known to look for dark water to hold. Structure can a great location to find protection, but some waters consist of only grassy banks, tall trees, or willows scattered along the river's edge. This bank structure will cast a shadow along the river's edge, drawing fish in. If you see a separate shadow along the edge of the main dark zone, there is a good chance it is a feeding fish.

SILHOUETTES

Problem: I cannot see any detailed targets.

Solution: Try looking for silhouettes of the trout's body, without an outline. The image will appear as greens, blues, purples, and grays.

Many often look into the water and try to locate a fish by searching for an entire trout complete with an outline. Often, they fail to see the fish directly in front of them.

The first and most important thing sight-fishers can do before hunting for the fish is build a reference in their mind of what the target will look like in the water. This is a great learning tool for improving every day you fish because you will begin looking for less obvious visual cues. You will then see more and larger trout.

For the best visual example, I tell clients to imagine a picture of a trout with a dark outline and detailed markings and color along the body. Now erase the outline and replace the detailed color and markings with water-colors of light blue or green. This is the subtle visual you want to keep in mind when look-ing for the silhouette of the trout below the surface. A silhouette is a rough, distorted, ghostly image that typically displays a light pastel shade of the trout's body color. I use the term "ghostly image" because every time I see a picture or video of a ghost, it has simi-lar features: a light white color and a hazy image without an outline.

When you are trying to distinguish between a trout and vegetation on the river bottom, remember that trout silhouettes take on a vague hue of blue, green, purple, or gray that is distinct from the river bottom.

Fresh rainbows like this one Bob Dye is releasing are difficult to see in deep holding runs. Try to target the vague blues and greens from the slight coloration above the trout's lateral line.

FIND FEEDING FISH

Problem: I keep casting to the fish, but it won't eat.

Solution: Determine whether the fish is feeding or sulking.

Let the trout's movements tell you if it is feeding. Then watch to see if it is lifting, dropping, moving side to side, or feeding on one side more than the other. If possible, look for the opening of the trout's mouth when it has performed what you think is a feeding movement. Just because the trout has moved does not mean it is feeding. When trout become conditioned to seeing movement (trout hunters) from above, they will no longer bolt when they spook out of a run. Instead, they will sulk and lay still on the river bottom. I give most trout the two-minute rule, counting to 120 while I watch the fish. If the trout doesn't feed, make a mental note of its location and return to try again in different light conditions.

While fish actively feeding in shallow water typically move from side to side, deep-water feeders take a more three-dimensional approach by also lifting and dropping. Deep-water fish lift because they see at a 45-degree angle in a cone projecting upward. They also drift backward in a last-minute hesitation and then perform a U-turn to feed. This is helpful to determine the depth you are going to set your rig at, knowing the actively feeding, moving fish will see it.

PATTERN FEEDING

Problem: I can't get the fish to take my fly with so many naturals on the surface.

Solution: Look for a pattern in the fish's surface-feeding behavior and time your flies to drift in view when the trout consumes its next meal.

I can't tell you how many times I've seen a fish take a natural bug on the surface and push my imitation away with the wake from the rise. When the opportunity presents itself, a trout will maximize how big its next meal will be. You can see this during a blan-ket, or complex, hatch in which the river's surface is covered with insects. During these hatches the trout can consume five naturals or more with every gulp.

Instead of looking for the next meal, fish begin to feed in patterns. They shave the surface two or three times and then rest for a second. You want to count the seconds in between each pause because that will let you know when and how fast you need to present your fly with the naturals so the fish takes them all at once. See the Hammering the Nail cast (page 107) for a quick and accurate cast. Lastly, make sure that you are not performing long drifts when you present the dry to pattern-feeding trout. Knowing that you may only have seconds after the fish rests before it feeds again, you need to place your bugs 12–24 inches above the feeding zone. This is the secret ingredient for increasing hookups during tough hatches like Tricos, which have small insects, and large, selective trout.

TARGET PRACTICE

Problem: I am having problems seeing the trout's body color below the water's surface.

Solution: Try looking for tail, belly, and fin colors.

Trout possess some of the most vibrant colors of any fish below the lateral line. Concentrate on the color from the lateral line up; this will let you know the tint the fish silhouettes will take.
JAY NICHOLS

nglers sight-fish based on detailed pictures they see in print. This seldom works, as it doesn't take into consideration the different colors trout take on for different seasons. Additionally, you must realize that when fishing you only see the fish from the lateral line up, not the entire fish. When anglers look for trout in the water, they are viewing from a 45-degree angle; the refraction of light tilts this angle upward to 32 degrees, making the belly of the trout less visible.

Look for colors that stand out against the river bottom. Most of the trout's camouflage is on its back, which is commonly blue or green. Red, yellow, and orange are contrasting colors that are easier to locate.

Different seasons supply different colors. For example, in the spring you will see more red, pink, and orange on rainbows, cuttbows, and cutthroats preparing to spawn. For the fall, yellow, orange, and pink are commonly found on brown and brook trout as they begin their migration.

In addition to matching color to season, you also want to look for specific body parts during each season. When hunting rainbows in the spring, most of the red and pink coloration is on the trout's gill plate and lateral line, making the front half the most visible part of the fish. Fall brings brown trout with more coloration on the belly in a line stretching from the dorsal fin to the tail. This makes hunting colored tails—not heads—the key to success.

A training tactic I used as a young adult was the "silver dollar" method. After this method was shown to me by a friend of the family, I would take a silver dollar and spray paint it red. In tough or slow fishing conditions I would take the red target and chuck it into various sections of the river, and then quickly turn my head away before it would land. I was then forced to search for the red object in the river. This training would later prove more valuable in my sight-fishing adventures than I ever could imagine.

SLICK-WATER WINDOWS

Problem: Turbulent water distorts the image, making it difficult to see anything below.

Solution: Try looking for "windows" of slick water moving in between turbulent water for viewing opportunities.

he best way to locate trout holding in locations that supply them with cover is to look for a transition in fast water of slick strips or "windows" that allow some visibility to the river bottom. Scan the viewing lane to locate the calm water above the area

Like rivers, still waters can also produce great windows of slick water between rolling waves and chop. I saw this chrome bow cruising through the window only a few feet below the reservoir's surface. PHILLIP TEREYLA

where you think the trout is holding, and find the widest window. Once you start noticing the smooth water above, you want to adjust your eyes to the speed at which the window is moving. Do this by following a few windows downstream without worrying about gazing into them. Finally follow the window as it moves, unfocus your eyes, and look for anything unnatural on the river bottom. Remember, when you locate the trout you are only going to get a quick glimpse of

the trout's body, normally the tail or the back. Even a glimpse will let you know how much line to drift in, how deep the trout is, and what direction it is facing.

Another method to window shopping is locating what you think is a trout below the water's surface. Keep your eyes locked on the potential prize, then, when a slick window floats over the presumed target, you will get a quick glimpse of what is below.

WAKES IN THE CALM

Problem: I have trouble seeing the fish in calm water with gray skies and heavy surface glare.

Solution: Try reading the surface to detect V wakes .

After seeing a few large wakes bolt off the banks as we drifted by, Eric Mondragon anchored the boat and carefully got into a tuck position to fish the numerous edge dwellers.

The easiest visual to see when fishing calm water with gray skies is the ring after a trout has sipped an insect off the surface. The problem is that this visual is what most trout hunters are looking for. But what if the ring doesn't appear? Is a trout still rising?

Reading water is one of those important basics in fly fishing, as it determines the best location and best current speed to fish. When you pay attention to the water's surface, you'll find it often indicates whether there are fish in the area. Look for rising trout beyond the calm water where they are easily seen. My favorite locations are riffled runs where other anglers do not easily see the trout because the trout's head or bulging back looks identical to the rolling bumps of the water's surface. The way to distinguish a trout from the water or a riffle bump is by the glint of light or body shine. The sun reflects off the mucus coating the trout's body. This will stand out against the rolling water that is not as bright.

Watch for wakes; by doing so, you can still enjoy the advantage of seeing in calm water beyond a riseform. I hunt the calm-water inlets to many stillwaters in search of the wakes left by the large trout pushing through the water below the surface. The advantage to watching wakes is you can determine the point when the wake stops.

This tells you the general area where the trout are holding and allows you to present to fish that other anglers don't detect. To increase your chances of success, try using streamers instead of drys or nymphs. This will let you cover a larger area when presenting to the fish and allow you to see the trout's wake if it tracks or moves to take the streamer. Always remember: sight-fishing is much more than just seeing the trout in the water. Paying attention to your surroundings—including the water's surface—can lead to great results.

JAW JACKING

Problem: I am having problems seeing the white of the fish's mouth to detect the strike.

Solution: Look for a jaw-jacking motion from the trout, like the fish is chewing gum.

When sight-fishing, a trout opening its mouth is a great indication that the trout is feeding. The problem is that the movement of a fish's mouth will be different once it has taken your fly. Knowing the difference between the two can help you determine if the fish has eaten a natural or if it has taken your imitation. This is all based on the jaw-jacking movements of the trout's mouth.

When a trout consumes a natural insect food source, it will typically open its mouth while its gills flare. This creates suction on top of, or below, the water's surface, allow-

ing the fish to consume its meal with one motion of open and closing its mouth. When trout are in a feeding frenzy, you'll see constant mouth movement that indicates the fish is actively feeding. The challenge is determining if the fish has taken your fly or the natural insect. The best indication that a fish has taken your fly is the chewing motion that follows the take as the fish feels an unnatural object in its mouth. The fish will immediately begin jacking its jaw like it is chewing on a piece of bubblegum while the imitation starts to dislodge from the trout's mouth.

When Phillip Tereyla spotted this fresh cuttbow, the large white opening of its mouth stood out against the dark bottom bay of the reservoir.

This jaw-jacking visual is important because the trout can spit the fly out before the indicator moves, meaning sight-fishing is our chance to take advantage of the roughly 40 percent of hits that you can't detect with a strike indicator.

SEVEN

Exceptional Casting

After twelve months of practice-casting almost every Saturday in the gym of Dougherty High School with my casting mentor Dusty Sprague, I completed one of my personal goals: to earn my casting certification from the Federation of Fly Fishers. The hours we spent filming our casting strokes and hands-on instruction taught me that manipulating the motion of your arm can result in accuracy over short distances as well as long.

This training served me best when I began to teach casting myself. To be the best guide possible, I had to be able to analyze everyone's casting and teach accordingly. This meant not only helping my clients become better casters, but also helping them fix the mistakes that they had already learned. Rule number one: you won't be a successful guide if your clients can't cast.

This was never more apparent than during a "Best of the West" competition at an International Sportsmen's Expo where I watched a few of the competitors break conventional casting strokes to get maximum flex out of their rod and achieve a cast of over 100 feet in such an unconventional manner. I wondered if it would be possible to just eliminate the false cast that commonly spooks trout.

While distance has its place, many scenarios that my clients and I encounter during our sight-fishing adventures don't require it. When you're working with only five feet of fly line, it is impossible to use the flex to properly load the rod. I realized that the movement of your arm in unison with your body keeps your line, leader, and tippet taut for straight-line presentations at a short distance that do not tangle or collapse.

This chapter teaches how to achieve short- and long-line presentations using unorthodox methods that will help prevent wary trout from spooking by seeing the cast or presentation.

ARM ROLL

Problem: I keep spooking fish with a false cast above the water where they are holding.

Solution: Try an arm-roll cast that places all the movement behind your body, not above the fish.

When you are in an intimate setting casting to a trout, false-casting with a two o'clock and ten o'clock rhythm can spook the trout as the line unrolls above their heads. To avoid this, allow your line to drift downstream lifted at a 45-degree angle until it is taut. Then roll your arm upstream and perform an aerial mend. This allows an accurate cast without all of the motion that may ruin the presentation before it even hits the water.

In many situations you are only dealing with a drift of five feet or less when you are presenting to a fish on the edge of the river or around structure, where this cast really shines. Knowing the drift will be short, if you do mend, there is a good chance you will pull the flies out of the trout's viewing lane. The arm-roll cast will perform the mend and allow you to focus on the trout during the drift, knowing that the take can happen fast.

Lastly, with 10-foot rods becoming popular for nymphing anglers, the arm-roll cast is very helpful, knowing it is the movement of your arm loading the rod, not the graphite. Many fly fishers have to learn these adjustments with 10-foot rods in close quarters because you simply cannot get the long graphite to load.

1. To start the arm-roll cast, load the rod from the tension of the fly line on the water's surface. Continue upward at a 45-degree angle downstream to get the maximum flex, storing energy in the rod. JAY NICHOLS PHOTOS

2. When the leader, flies, and tippet are clear of the water, allow the fly line to unroll taut while you start the rolling rotation of your arm. Keep your forearm and wrist straight.

3. Roll your arm down to the side and upstream of the trout. This will continue the casting stroke and prevent the fish from detecting the fly line.

4. Allow the line to unroll in front of you while you drop the rod tip to your upstream side. The result is a proper presentation with a reach mend above the trout. This eliminates the need to mend, avoids disturbing the water, and eliminates any movement above the trout.

CASTING FROM A BROKEN WRIST

Problem: I need to shoot numerous feet of line quickly without a false cast.

Solution: Try breaking your wrist on the back cast to generate more line speed on the forward casting sroke.

Many casting instructors teach anglers not to break their wrists during the cast. Breaking your wrist prevents the rod tip from traveling in a straight plane, and most importantly, can create tailing loops on the back and forward casting stokes. While this is true, many anglers don't realize the benefits of breaking their wrists to create power during the casting stroke. They lose the chance to make a quick cast that can shoot numerous feet of line with one back and forward cast.

I realized the benefits of breaking your wrist on the backcast while watching those Best of the West distance-casting championships at the International Sportsmen's Expo. Some of the competitors would use what looked to me like an incorrect backcast—then they would make a 115-foot cast with a 5-weight rod. The sheer power they were storing in the rod made it possible to cast so far.

Here's how it works: When you pull the rod back on the backward casting stroke, briefly pause the tip at two o'clock and allow a tight loop to begin rolling behind you.

Then, instead of keeping the rod in this position, allow your arm to drift back while you begin to break your wrist. Stop the rod at three o'clock, with the rod tip pointed straight behind you. Once you reach the flat-rod position, stop and begin the forward cast by rolling your wrist forward until the rod is back in the straight plane of two o'clock. Then push the rod forward on the front casting stroke while performing a haul. Stop at ten o'clock in front of you, and then extend the bend from breaking and rolling your wrist and match that with a haul. Stop abruptly at ten o'clock in front of you. The rod will bend so aggressively it looks like it is going to snap, and low-quality graphite will do just that.

This method provides a huge advantage when using streamers or casting heavy nymph rigs in tight quarters or when you need to cover a lot of ground without over-casting and spooking fish. When using streamers you can strip line into the bank pickup with one broken wrist backcast and shoot 20–30 feet with one single casting stroke.

1. Starting with your line taut behind you on the backcast, allow your wrist to break with the rod at the two o'clock position. To visualize the proper position of the wrist, imagine you are holding a baseball bat with the top of the bat resting on your shoulder. JAY NICHOLS PHOTOS

2. Push the rod straight forward with your elbow at your side. At the same time push your thumb straight forward like you are trying to pinch your index finger through the cork handle of the rod. You wrist will roll and "break" forward, increasing the speed and power of your cast.

3. Stop the rod at ten o'clock on the forward cast in the direction of where you want to present your rig. A tight loop will begin to unroll in front of you.

4. If you cast correctly, the line and loop will travel at maximum speed, without any shockwaves in the line from power being applied too early or too late in the cast.

5. Keep the rod at ten o'clock until the fly line has straightened out and begins to fall to the water's surface.

HAMMERING THE NAIL

Problem: In heavy wind, my cast collapses and blows back to me.

Solution: Try mimicking the motion of hammering a nail during your cast.

Learning the basics and relying on just one method to perform a cast (e.g., the two o'clock to ten o'clock method) can make proper presentation difficult in foul weather and short-distance situations. In heavy wind, for example, anglers using too much power still find their leader collapsing in front of them, destroying any chance at accuracy.

The rod tip should travel on a straight plane every time you make a cast. If you mimic the motion of hammering a nail—with your elbow tucked to your side—the casting stroke will drive to the surface of the water from twelve o'clock to nine o'clock. This allows your leader to straighten out even in the worst conditions of 30 mph-plus winds and gives you more accuracy in short-line situations.

Another advantage to hammering the nail is you can use this method in the forward part of the casting stoke and still perform a false cast behind you. The key is making sure the rod tip stops at 12 o'clock above you so the rod tip drives straight down to the water in a straight plane. If the tip travels back to 2 o'clock the direction of the rod tip will bow, losing energy when it rolls forward.

1. Start with the rod tip directly above you at twelve o'clock or slightly back. This will leave the fly line draped on the water's surface in line with your arm for a proper load. JAY NICHOLS PHOTOS

2. With your elbow to your side, begin mimicking the motion of hammering a nail, dropping the rod tip straight down. The tension of the fly line on the water's surface will flex the rod, supplying power for the cast.

3. Continue with smooth acceleration of the rod tip straight down and in a straight angled plane. The line will roll off the water's surface and form a tight, forward-moving loop, giving you distance and accuracy in the cast.

4. With the fly line, leader, and tippet traveling above the water you will have less disturbance on the surface. Continue the hammering motion down.

5. By pointing at the fly line straight, your cast will end with great accuracy and with the rod tip just above the water's surface.

Notice the distance Trevor has between his non-casting hand and his casting hand. This gives him more range of motion to extend his cast.

HOLDING LINE

Problem: In short-line situations I am losing loops and power on the back and forward strokes.

Solution: Stop holding line in your non-casting hand. This allows more drifting length in the back and forward cast.

Beginner fly fishers can fall into the habit of holding line when they cast, leading to the loss of power, accuracy, and speed. Yes, there are situations when managing line in the non-casting hand is an effective means of generating line speed, such as the double haul when you are casting more than 30 feet. However, in short-line situations it can be a difficult habit to break.

I teach clients to get used to casting and controlling the drift using only the casting hand. This helps you feel the weight of the fly line when it is flexing the graphite rod and storing energy. Once you can perform straight presentations, allow your non-casting hand to come into play for managing line after the cast.

When you are false-casting or picking up and laying down line, holding fly line in your non-dominant hand prevents you from having drifting distance on your backcast. This occurs because the hand holding the line cannot break the plane of your chest or shoulder, essentially cutting your backcast distance in half. You need the distance to drift back with an abrupt pause to generate line speed, allowing you to have more power and distance in the forward casting stroke.

OPEN AND CLOSE THE FRIDGE DOOR

Problem: My line keeps collapsing and tangling from tailing loops.

Solution: Pretend you are opening and closing a refrigerator door to maintain a straight path of the rod tip.

The two biggest problems I see in anglers' casting strokes are too much power when trying to force the rod and breaking the wrist (without the goal of achieving maximum distance), which saps any stored power from the flexing rod. Both of these habits will cause the line to collapse during the cast and create tailing loops where the fly line mimics an animal's tail looping over itself. This causes knots and tangles. You want to think of the casting stroke as a pulling and pushing motion, which allows the graphite in the rod time to flex. This maintains the bend in the forward and backcast. Stopping the rod then releases the built-up energy.

When I teach on the water, I come up with analogies that match the everyday motions people use, giving my clients an automatic visual and physical connection to the technique. For false-casting, I use the example of opening and closing a fridge door. You pull back the fridge door to an abrupt stop, and then you push the door forward to close it. This same motion also helps an angler keep his or her wrist locked, preventing it from breaking during the casting and losing the flex in the rod. Lastly, when you do pull open and push close the fridge door, make sure your elbow is to your side and down. It is common for anglers, especially beginning anglers, to lift their arms and fully extend them while they cast, to resemble a throwing motion. This will cause your arm to tire out and prevent the rod from traveling in a straight plane in the front- and backcasts. Once you get used to pulling the cast back and pushing it forward with smooth acceleration to an abrupt stop with a slight pause behind you and in front of you, you will see immediate results with the cast. This technique allows my clients to perform the presentation right away with good results on the river.

PICK UP AND LAY DOWN

Problem: I don't know when the rod is loading.

Solution: Use a pick-up and lay-down cast to feel the flex and load of the rod.

When I tested for my casting certification from the Federation of Fly Fishers in 2002, the goal was to become an efficient casting instructor and to improve daily success for my clients during guide trips. I wanted clients to leave with the correct habits that would allow them to grow as anglers so that if they returned for another guide trip, they would have more skills and increased odds for success. Many anglers struggle because they learn how to cast on grass and not on the river. We had anglers false-casting over and over again, scaring the trout with all that motion above and disturbance on the river surface.

We immediately began performing our casting lessons on the river's edge with the lines in the water so people knew how to load from the line tension on the water's surface. I started teaching the pick-up and lay-down cast before I let anglers begin false-casting on the river. This teaches my clients how to make a cast and a drift to present again on the next casting stroke. It also

One of the most effective ways to load a rod with a backcast is by using the tension of the water to store power in the graphite. The pick-up and lay-down cast will load the line on the water's surface. By stopping at twelve o'clock, it will straighten out behind the angler loading the forward casting stroke. This eliminates unnecessary movement above the trout and disturbance on the surface.

teaches them how to manage the line lying on the water's surface when they get ready to start fishing. When anglers false-cast every time, the ripping line on the water's surface spooks most of the trout in front of them. Lastly, the rod loading from the pulling of the water's surface is more dramatic than the load from the weight of the fly line in the air. This helps the student feel when they are storing the right amount of power in the rod. When these anglers started achieving distance, the double or single haul is easier to

perform because they feel an increase in line speed and power in the cast.

To perform this cast, start with your rod tip just above the water's surface and your fly line laid out in front of you while drifting downstream in the current. Then, with smooth acceleration, lift the rod to a twelve o'clock or one o'clock position with an abrupt stop. This acceleration will form a large bend in your rod, storing energy. After a slight pause with the line, leader, and tippet taut behind you, push the rod tip forward with smooth acceleration to an abrupt stop—again storing energy—and release the line forward with a tight, unrolling loop. This gives you a straight-line presentation. The key to teaching this cast is not allowing the angler to return the rod tip to the water's surface on the forward stroke; doing so causes disturbance. You want to use soft lands on the line, leader, and fly as they fall from the ten o'clock rod position.

ROLL WITH A HAUL

Problem: I can't achieve enough distance with my conventional roll cast.

Solution: Try a single haul on the forward motion of the casting stroke for maximum line speed.

The ideal way to generate line speed when performing a roll cast is through creating moving tension of the line. To do this, skate the line on the water surface as you lift your rod to a starting point on the forward stroke. In many situations on rivers and stillwaters, the movement of the line before the abrupt stop leading to the forward casting stroke doesn't have enough tension to achieve distance on the cast.

Similar to a double haul with a normal casting stroke, a single haul before the forward stroke on a roll cast will increase line speed and allow you to get a maximum rod load for the distance. To perform the roll cast with a haul, start the cast with your rod tip in front of you as you would for the end of a drift or presentation. Then, with smooth acceleration, lift your rod to the one o'clock position with the line hanging behind your shoulder in a D shape. Once you reach this position, make sure you pause before performing the forward casting stoke. This will allow the line to create more tension and load the rod. Then, with the line in your non-casting hand, push your rod forward with smooth acceleration at the same time you pull (haul) 6 to 12 inches of line and immediately release it. Abruptly stop the rod at ten o'clock and leave the angle of the rod tip forward but high enough to shoot line. This is where you can use the "closing the fridge door" motion to match the position and movement of the forward cast. The increase in line speed will allow you to shoot up to 40 feet of line on both moving waters and stillwaters.

When roll-casting on stillwaters, do not pause too long at twelve o'clock. Make sure the line is still moving toward you when performing the maneuver. If you don't, it inhibits line speed.

1. Position the rod just above the water's surface, giving you vertical clearance for the cast. Hold a generous amount of line below the index (trigger) finger of your rod hand to achieve distance at the end of the cast. JAY NICHOLS PHOTOS

2. With smooth acceleration, start lifting the rod to a vertical position. Keep the rod tip in line with your shoulder during the lift.

3. Keep the rod tip traveling back until you reach the one o'clock position, then abruptly stop the rod. The line will continue to move on the water's surface after the rod stops. This will provide tension in the rod for the forward cast.

4. Begin pushing the rod forward in a straight plane with powerful acceleration. Hold the line in your non-casting hand, and release the line under the index finger of your casting hand.

5. Continue accelerating forward by pushing the rod. At the same time pull down the line in your opposite hand one to two feet. This will create a haul and generate more line speed for power in the cast.

6. Allow the line to travel freely through your non-casting hand, and abruptly stop the rod when it points to nine o'clock in the direction you want to present. The increased line speed and maximum flex in the rod will shoot the remaining slack line, giving you better distance in the cast.

TENSION CAST

Problem: My conventional cast creates too much movement above the water's surface.

Solution: Use line tension to keep the rod loaded for only a forward cast to present the flies.

When you perform a roll cast with a forward stroke, or when you leave your line hanging in the water while attempting to sight-fish, you create enough disturbances to ruin any stealth movement. A tension cast can prevent this. Start at the bottom of a run, and then lift your rod to a twelve o' clock position to give tension to the line, leader, and tippet. Bring your rod in a downward motion (hammering a nail) to nine o'clock, giving you a straight presentation with power, as well as no unnecessary movement that might spook fish.

This cast is money when you are hunting a fair distance of water, or trying to creep into position to cast to a trout you see. The ground you cover is endless as long as the rod remains at twelve (loaded) and the line gets tension while riding on the river's surface. Speed plays a big role when delivering the mail to large trout. You may only get three casts before the fish detect you or something unnatural. The tension cast is the quickest way to present a straight rig upstream of the fish.

When faced with fast water and no room for a backcast, you can load the rod by creating tension through the fly line on the water's surface. This was a helpful technique for achieving distance on the Gunnison River's East Portal in Colorado. JAY NICHOLS

TUCKING INTO TIGHT QUARTERS

Problem: I can't present my flies in tight quarters and around structure.

Solution: Tuck your rig into a tight spot with your flies landing first.

Anglers miss opportunities when they employ traditional casting methods in situations that require an unconventional technique. This goes for narrow strips of open water in between rocks or small pockets of open water in vegetation-filled runs.

When fishing in tight quarters, I manipulate the movement of my arm, body, and rod position to present when the line cannot load the rod at such a short distance. This is especially important around structure because these situations leave little room for error if the cast is off. You will simply lose your rig to a snag and ultimately spook the fish.

My favorite structure to hunt is in between rocks where the strip of open water supplies a holding zone for the trout. The fish's vision is blocked, like that of an angler standing at the bottom of canyon walls. This allows you to sneak in from the side and get close to the target, sometimes within a rod's length. To get the right drift, the fly or flies—not the fly line or strike indicator—have to land first. This will allow everything on your rig to drift in a straight plane downstream between the rocks.

The tuck cast is the best way to make this accurate presentation. Start with the rod extended straight in front of your body. Then, with smooth acceleration, roll the tip of the rod in a counterclockwise circular motion, around three feet in diameter. When the rod tip is three quarters of the way around this imaginary circle, abruptly stop the tip and keep it in place. This allows the line, leader, and rig to continue through the full circle and eventually land in the river. The abrupt stop will kick the line back, causing the flies to enter the water first, followed by the leader, and finally by the fly line.

When using the tuck cast, a 10-foot rod can add an advantage, as it provides more reach and distance. This allows for a stealthier cast and greater maneuverability in conditions that have a large amount of structure.

1. Point your rod tip and arm straight out in front of your body downstream of the target. Use the straight arm to lift the rod downstream and up at a 45-degree angle. JAY NICHOLS PHOTOS

2. Make a counterclockwise circular motion using a straight arm. Your rod tip should travel in a circle with a diameter of about three feet. The fly line will remain taut during the cast.

3. Continue the circular counterclockwise motion with smooth acceleration.

4. Once the rod tip reaches about the ten o'clock position above the target zone, abruptly stop the rod with a straight arm and allow the fly line to continue traveling downward.

5. This will drive the fly (or flies) into the water with accuracy, while the rod tip remains at the ten o'clock position. Keep a straight arm and mimic the position of a high-stick, allowing your rig to plummet quickly toward the river bottom.

WATER-LOAD CAST

Problem: I have problems casting when I am wading in an area that has no room for a backcast.

Solution: Create a forward cast using tension from the water's surface downstream.

It is sometimes impossible to reach the opposite bank of a wide river with a backcast or roll cast, even when you are wading as far out in the water as you can.

A water load of the fly line is an effective way to overcome this and to store power in your rod for long-distance presentations. On the backcast, angle your line downstream towards the area where the length of the fly line will land on the water. Then, without letting it sink too far, bring your rod tip forward from a three o'clock position behind you. By pushing the rod tip forward and stopping at ten o'clock you will get a maximum flex from the rod when you roll your wrist forward from the rod straight behind you. In addition to the tension of all the line ripping off the water's surface, this can be used effectively with floating, intermediate-sinking, and full-sinking lines.

When heavier nymph rigs, streamers, or drys are behind you, make sure your tip is horizontal with the plane of the water's surface. From that position push forward upstream or across river. This is similar to breaking your wrist to get maximum load and shoot more line. Do not, however, come forward by rolling your arm; instead, push your arm in the direction of the cast. This allows for more accuracy.

1. Start the water-load cast by facing the line placed behind you and at a downstream angle. The rod should be straight and pointed at the fly line just above the water's surface.

JAY NICHOLS PHOTOS

2. Elevate the rod to a two o'clock position to create tension on the fly line from the water's surface. Begin rotating your body in the direction of the forward casting stroke.

3. Continue the rod tip on a straight path forward, with your body facing toward the area where you want to cast.

4. Using smooth acceleration, continue pushing the rod tip forward toward the ten o'clock position. This will give maximum flex and power to the fly rod.

5. Abruptly stop the rod at ten o'clock. This will release the power stored in the rod. By keeping the tip traveling in a straight plane, you will form a tight loop that will shoot all the line accurately to the target area.

Water loading a cast can also be effective with your line in front of you and no water behind. This angler is demonstrating this technique in the Arctic Circle in Alaska.

chapter EIGHT

Presenting to the Trout

One of my most eye-opening experiences concerning presentation on the water took place in 2008 during a trip with Eric Mondragon, Jay Harper, and Shannon Harper to the Arctic Circle in search of giant arctic char and Dolly Varden. During my time guiding and fishing in Alaska, there were sometimes simply so many fish that it seemed like catching rather than fishing. Well, nothing could have been further from the truth during our Arctic Circle hunt for pink-bellied giants. When we arrived, the water was lower and clearer than normal and the char were wary. The sinking-tip lines and full-sink lines we arrived with in anticipation of a deep, wide river were not going to cut it. We instead reverted to the floating lines, 15-foot leaders, and weighted flies that we used daily on our home waters.

The original plan was to take two loads each for two anglers with half the gear on each trip to our destination. Since my luggage had been lost in Chicago by the airline, this changed to two loads total: one of anglers with minimal gear followed by a load with the main gear. While waiting in Kotzebue sorting through this dilemma, we tried to get information from the local fish and game office. Fortunately, the secretary's boyfriend was a local charter pilot who had seen a school of the fish recently. Making a last-minute change of plans, we were dropped on a tributary and, while waiting for the bulk of our gear, began to wet-wade. (Yes, this was the coldest water I had ever stuck my feet into!) The fish had moved out of the main river and into this small tributary, so presentation was key. With movement from above spooking the char, we began to sight-fish from a kneeling position with a floating line attached to a single Meat Whistle. Had we not tried such an unusual presentation, we never would have landed the over 20-pound fish that we all took turns catching.

I have always said presentation is more important than fly selection. This chapter embodies that philosophy and goes beyond typical methods of presentation to explore simpler and more effective techniques.

STEALTH STEPS

Problem: While maneuvering around the river and trying to position myself for a perfect cast, I end up spooking fish.

Solution: Try diving and sliding your boots into a better casting position.

While shallow-water wading situations may seem easy as far as movement, it can be challenging to prevent noise and vibrations every time you step into the water's surface. Because your steps will cause a splash, fish will feel or see the noise and vibrations. To overcome this challenge, you must dive your feet as they enter the water to prevent a disturbance on the water's surface. This mimics the movements made by fish-hunting birds. One of the best species to watch displaying this technique is the great blue heron. While standing in two feet of water, herons walk along the river's edge and gracefully step in and out of the water without creating any disturbance, allowing them to creep into a position to feed on the trout or baitfish along the river's edge. Mimicking these movements by diving your foot with every step you take will allow you to get into position to present to a trout without creating a disturbance and allow you to stay out of view by staying in a low tucked or hunched over position.

To begin the dive, you first want to make sure that when you are moving upstream in a forward wading motion or you are moving sideways as you face forward, you do not cross your feet every time you take a step. This will allow you to maintain balance while you concentrate on diving your feet to prevent commotion. Then, with every step you should lift your boot completely out of the water, extend your leg in the direction you are moving, and reenter your boot into the water with your toes pointing straight down. This will allow your foot to enter the water without creating a splash like you would if your foot was flat. Try to imagine your foot as an Olympic diver entering a pool after bouncing off the diving board. When you are wading in this fashion, you only want to extend your leg two to three feet with each step to allow the direction of your boot to remain straight down towards the river's bottom and not down at an angle, like you'd do if you were to extend farther than three feet. This birdlike posture will allow you more shots at shallow dwelling targets.

Trying to battle fast water with forceful steps can spook wary trout from the commotion below the water's surface. By sliding your feet just above the river bottom with long, slow strides, you can minimize vibration and noise, allowing you to get into better casting range and position. Move in a forward direction, letting the front (and thinnest) part of your legs move through the water because it will create less resistance when you move your leg. Keep your boot just above the river bottom and slowly slide it forward until it is fully extended in front of you.

Then, plant your foot down, making sure you do not stir up the river bottom and create more vibrations and noise than necessary. Perform the same movement with your other leg, preventing your boots from hitting one another by keeping your legs six to twelve inches apart. This will help you with balance and prevent noise below the water's surface if your feet touch or your pant legs slide against one another. Unlike a normal step made when you are wading (where you lift your knee up then extend your foot down), you want your legs to remain as straight as possible while you extend your feet forward to prevent any disturbance on the water's surface. It is as if you are trying to mimic a knife slicing through the water every time you make a step. While it is a slow process, you can still cover a good deal of water by extending your slide as you move.

DEFEATING VEGETATION

Problem: I am having problems fishing in vegetation.

Solution: Switch to a topwater bite with attractors like hoppers, poppers, and mice.

Fall is the best time to target early migratory browns, but it can be a challenge to present subsurface imitations amid the overgrowth of vegetation that results from low water flows. In fact, some of the vegetation can grow all the way to the surface of the water, making it impossible to get a subsurface drift of any kind.

Brown trout love vegetation for the cover it supplies and the food that calls these vegetation blankets home. When you know the trout will find comfort anywhere veg grows, more of the river opens up to presentations using topwater imitations. Hoppers and mice can be the ticket to luring trout out of these congested areas of the river.

Start by targeting low-light situations when trout begin to move out of protected areas as the light disappears and shadows or movement cannot be detected. My favorite times for low light are two hours before dark and when the skies turn black with the promise of rain. You can then begin searching with flies that ride low in the film to create a waking disturbance that will get the giants' attention. Some of my go-to flies are #8-14 Morrish Mouse, #10-14 Fat Albert, and #10-14 Redleg Hoppers. Mimic the searching method you would use with a streamer by walking down- or upriver three to five feet at a time, casting to the opposite bank and letting the fly swing to the bank you are standing on. You can see the wake in the heavy glare created by stormy skies, or near nightfall when the water surface looks like a glass road covered in black ice. This will allow you

to see and stay connected with the fly and know when the fish takes.

Sections of the river will have open pockets scattered through deep runs and often around log or rock structures. These pockets give you deep access to present nymphs and streamers to trout that hold there waiting to ambush their next meal. Make sure your flies sink quickly. Don't use a stripping retrieve with streamers; instead, jig the fly to produce movement in the open pocket. The ideal scenario is to have the tip of your rod directly above your flies to keep tension to your leader and give you the ability to lift and drop your flies immediately to create movement and prevent snags.

I can tell you firsthand the saying "happy wife, happy life" is true! My lovely wife Michelle cradles a beautiful brown that was hiding in the vegetation.

NOT DRAG-FREE

Problem: I can't get a drag-free drift in a particular area.

Solution: Try swinging to success.

Many anglers learn that the best way to drift is to allow your flies to drift naturally in the current. The most common way to achieve a drag-free drift is with a mend, in which you place the fly line and leader upstream of the flies to remove tension and let them sink. This works well in deep water that supplies room for the flies to sink but can be frustrating in shallow water where you begin snagging structure or river bottom.

I think the term "drag-free drift" is misleading. Yes, your indicator or line is drifting drag-free, but the flies below the surface still create drag by moving around in the turbulent current. Drifting your flies to supply tension to the presentation can solve the problem of snagging the river bottom because the constant tension will keep your rig in the middle of the water column.

In shallow-water settings, a swing method works well because you can have the imitation accurately pass through the trout's viewing lane at a 45-degree angle and drift short past the trout, preventing snags or foul-hooking the fish. This will often make the trout turn and commit to eat before the meal disappears. This is also a great way to control depth in shallow water as the flies will ride higher in the water column when swinging and allow feeding trout a better view of the bugs.

In deep-water scenarios—whether you are using a standard nymph rig or a Czech-style nymph rig—you can elevate your rod and leader setup to keep tension to your rig and drift just above the river bottom without snags. For the best connection during the presentation, lead the flies with the tip of your rod to supply a 45-degree angle to your imitation. This stiff tension will also help you feel any subtle takes. When supplying tension, keep in mind that your leader length should increase no matter how you build it, and removing any strike indicator will allow a more intimate connection with the river bottom. You will get many takes at the end of the swing when you begin lifting for the next cast.

John Barr displays a large Yampa River rainbow that fell victim to a Drowned Trico swung with tension in a large back eddy.

MOVEMENT DRIFT

Problem: Many fly fishers believe that all drifts should be free of movement.

Solution: Try adding movement to a drift for better accuracy.

Jay Nichols stalks a quality rainbow on the Frying Pan River using drag to give the drift movement. A true advantage to using tension is immediately feeling the take.

Some learn only the basics of fly fishing, including the importance of a movement-free drift. While a natural drift will help you achieving depth and get an extension of a drift, it can also prevent you from experimenting with drift that supplies movement to get a trout to take. Imparting this movement to your rig can help you accurately place your flies to ensure they enter the trout's viewing lane.

In subsurface conditions, in both slow- and fast-moving water, your flies move from the speed of the water and don't drift drag-free. Being aware of this natural movement and applying your own manipulation can lead to success in areas of the river where shallow water drops quickly into a deep run.

When I present to fish in deep water where the drop line from the shallow water at the head of the run is immediate, I overweight my rig for the deep-water setting rather than shallow water. Then, after landing the flies two to three feet upstream of the drop line, I will twitch my flies with quick, one- to two-foot sideways movements with the tip of the fly rod. This moves my flies into the middle of the river column and lifts them back into position before they have a chance to snag bottom. This technique lets me deliver flies in deep-water settings without worrying about the interruption of a shallow drop at the head of the run.

You can also apply this movement for accuracy using every discipline. I draw an imaginary line from the trout's head upstream to where my flies should land (similar to a golfer when lining up his putt). This gives me the confidence of knowing my flies will enter the trout's viewing lane instead of guessing on each drift. If I cast past this imaginary line, I can twitch my flies back on track. If the fish are looking up in a prime feeding temperature of 55–65 degrees and a large fish is nestled right along the bank, making it tough to get a drag-free drift, I cast slightly above the trout. Once the imitation enters the viewing lane, applying a twitch can entice the fish to come out of the cover and take the fly.

SEEING MORE STRIKES

Problem: I am having problems detecting takes when using an indicator.

Solution: Use tension in your drift to detect and feel subtle movements.

I am a big fan of using tension when I am presenting my flies. The leader, tippet, and flies below the surface move with tension in the current. By using more swing-style drifts with tension and making less aggressive mends, you will see more takes through the indicator.

Another way to catch more fish is by looking for the subtle movements of the indicator, not just an aggressive bump. I am a big fan of Thingamabobbers because the indicator comes in various sizes and requires no maintenance. When using yarn or other standard indicators you need to comb out and apply floatant throughout the day. When I am tracking a Thingamabobber, I look for a pause, bump, and a twist or slide of the indicator to let me know a trout has taken my flies below. You become a better sight-fisher by looking for every detail. It is not just about seeing the trout—it is about seeing the details in every aspect of fishing.

Another advantage to drifting with tension or less aggressive mends is the straight line accuracy you get from the fly line through the leader and tippet. It builds confidence knowing that your rig is tracking in the same direction as the fish's viewing lane. You can see subtle movements in the fly line and feel the take when you are not using an indicator.

UNDERCUT BANKS

Problem: I can't get a good drift under an undercut bank.

Solution: Swing your flies under the bank at a 45-degree angle.

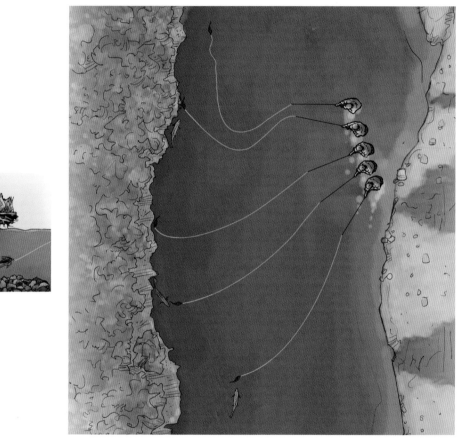

Using tension when you present flies gives you control over the presentation. This is helpful in circumstances like undercut banks because even a few inches can be the difference between a snag and an effective drift. JOE MAHLER

Undercut banks are some of the best locations for large trout to hold and feed because the trout will have maximum protection or cover. For years anglers have targeted these areas, but conventional drag-free drifts simply do not get the flies deep into the undercut where the trout are holding.

As with many other presentations, I have found confidence over the years using a taut line. I swing my flies into the undercut and allow the large trout to see my offering. To perform a proper swing, start by casting above the undercut at a 45-degree angle with your fly landing as close to the bank as possible. Then throw a downstream mend to position the fly line straight along the bank in the downstream direction. This becomes the excess line that will swing into the undercut. When the flies drift into the first opening of water in the undercut bank, twitch the tip of the rod back about one foot toward the bank nearest you. This straightens out the fly line, creating an extended line that is now upstream from the early mend downstream. Your flies will ultimately extend two to three feet into the undercut bank, allowing your subsurface presentations of nymphs and streamers to be effective.

If you can't swing the flies under the bank, try to trigger a take by drifting right next to the bank. Often, a drop-off or shadow will provide cover. Always look at the current upstream from the undercut and read where the drift comes into the run. Remember to cast short.

Your attractor fly can entice the target to move out of its comfort zone, especially during low-light conditions. Sometimes even the most stubborn fish will investigate an attractor streamer.

PROPER HOPPER

Problem: Twitching my hopper is not working.

Solution: Overshoot the target and mend to cause disturbance, followed by a movement-free drift.

Some believe that when you are fishing big imitations, like hoppers and mice, you should always skate the fly along the surface by pulling line or twitching the rod. Yes, this can entice big trout to take, but always remember that large trout are lazy by nature and that while they will eat a large meal, they prefer a food supply that isn't escaping. Also, a hopper's natural movement is that it falls on the water's surface; while there is some fluttering of the body and legs, most of the time hoppers lie still with their legs extended.

I get the best results with big attractor drys by applying movement at the beginning of the drift, followed by a drag-free drift. To achieve this I overshoot the target by a foot or two. Then, with an aggressive shoot mend that moves the fly 6–12 inches, I place all of my fly line upriver of the fly. This causes disturbance and moves the fly without it lifting off the water's surface. After the mend, I point the tip of my rod at the fly line and gain back any unnecessary slack line to ensure a proper set. This is a great technique for triggering a take and getting the trout to

My daughter Madelyn quickly learned the effectiveness of hoppers on the river's edge during windy afternoons on the South Platte River.

eat the fly as it comes to investigate the hopper that is pausing and riding drag-free.

Sometimes you have only a short drift when presenting your fly because you are wading in tight quarters or you are passing edges quickly while drifting. In these scenarios, you should replace the aggressive mend with a heavy slap followed by a drag-free drift. This will often surprise or startle edge-dwelling fish and trigger a feeding response.

THE "JOHNNY CASH"

Problem: My slow-strip streamer technique is not effective.

Solution: Try making a fast, erratic movement similar to strumming a guitar.

The biggest challenge in fishing streamers is mixing up your retrieve and making sure the motion you supply in the strip with your hand is transferred through to also move the fly. Many anglers will simply pull line from underneath their index finger, slowly stripping the line back without any erratic movement. This will not supply the abrupt movement that a streamer needs to make it look like it is injured or escaping.

When fishing streamers I tell anglers the best way to generate power in a strip of line without exceeding the proper length requires the same motion as strumming a guitar. With your thumb, middle, and index fingers, grab the fly line behind the index finger of the opposite hand. By mimicking the strum of a guitar with a pick, you flick your wrist down to strip 3–6 inches of line. (You can increase this to a 12-inch strip if needed.) This fast, erratic motion will give a jiglike effect to the streamer, causing it to pulsate and undulate and trigger an aggressive take by the trout. This is also helpful when you need to get the most action out of a retrieve in narrow water where long, fast strips would pull the fly out of the trout's viewing lane too fast. The short "strumming" strips will give life to even the shortest distances.

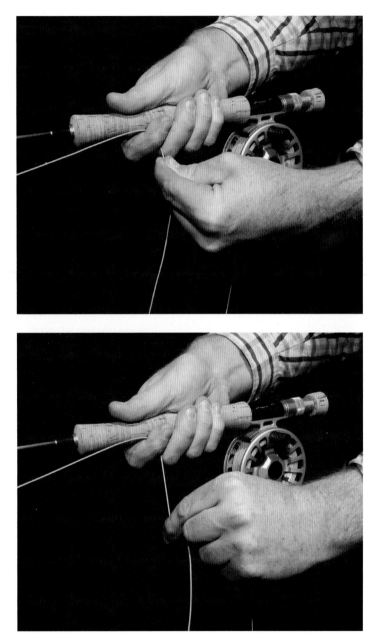

1. After the cast, place the fly line under the index finger of your casting hand. Then take your thumb and index finger of your non-casting hand and pinch the fly line.

2. Rotate your wrist downward in a motion that mimics strumming a guitar with a pick in the same fingers with your non-casting hand. At the same time, loosen your grip on the line below the index finger of your casting hand to ensure smooth line movement.

3. Once you've fully rotated your wrist, flick your fingers down and open them at the same time. This will shoot an extra inch or two in the retrieve, and impart great movement to the streamer.

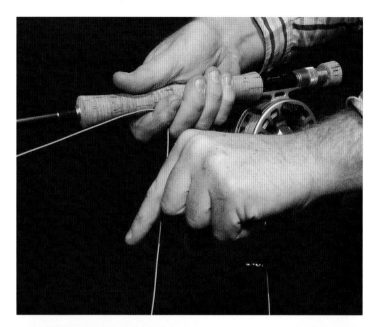

4. Pinch the fly line with the index finger of your casting hand. Reposition the middle and index fingers of your non-casting hand on the fly line and pinch. Repeat the process many times for an effective retrieve.

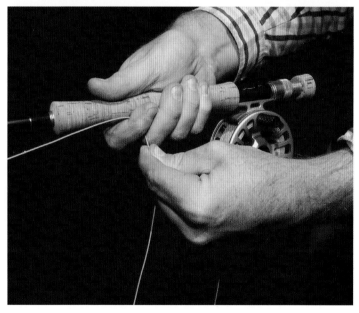

THE STRIP-AND-GIVE

Problem: Fish are chasing my streamer to the bank without taking.

Solution: Make sure your retrieve keeps the streamer in a prime feeding location while appearing injured.

Those who fish streamers on a regular basis sometimes have frustrating encounters where the trout will repeatedly chase a streamer to the river's edge without a take. Some fly fishers believe the problem is in the presentation or in the fly, but I wanted to dig deeper than that. I have a theory for why some trout will not commit—and how to fool them into doing so.

Trout want to commit but they hesitate to do so outside of comfortable, covered locations with deep water and structure. On most rivers there are three types of lies in which trout hold: shelter, prime, and feeding. All of these locations can supply quality fish, but the prime and shelter lies are often deep with less turbulent water, like that at the head of a run (where the feeding lie is located). Create a retrieve that supplies movement and accuracy while the fly remains in the fish's prime holding area.

Start by casting downstream at a 45-degree angle to the other side of the river or hole. Place your rod tip at the water surface and turn your body downstream as your line begins to swing into the holding zone. Once your streamer enters the trout's viewing lane, perform a conventional strip. Your fly line should be under the index finger of your dominant hand that is holding the cork of the rod. Then, by grasping line with your other hand, pull a few inches or feet of fly line to supply movement to the fly. Instead of pinching line with your casting hand's index finger and performing another strip of line, allow the river's current to pull back (give) the line you just retrieved. Continue with the same motion for every strip-and-give, working with the same length of fly line and keeping it in the holding zone.

1. Start with the rod tip just above the water's surface at a downward angle. Pinch the fly line under the index finger of your casting hand. With the thumb, index, and middle fingers of the non-casting hand, grip the fly line just below the index finger of the casting hand.

2. Loosen the grip below the index finger of your casting hand while you strip back 6 to 12 inches of line with the thumb, index, and middle fingers of your non-casting hand. At the same time, repeatedly wiggle the rod tip side-to-side 2 to 3 inches at a time until the strip stops.

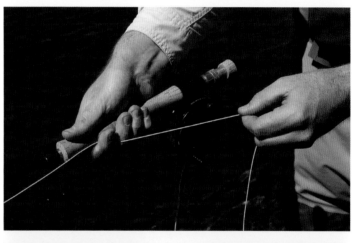

3. Release the grip under the index finger of your casting hand while the fly line is still in the same position with the opposite hand after the strip.

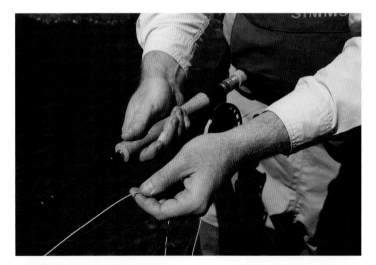

4. Allow your non-casting hand—still with a firm grip on the fly line—to move forward at the same speed the fly line is being pulled by the river's current. Stop the motion with your non-casting hand just in front of the cork handle of the fly rod.

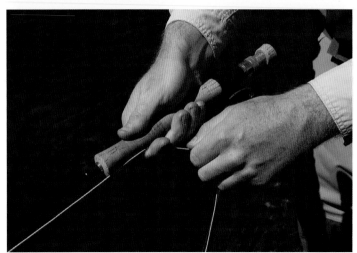

5. Repeat step number one, and allow the streamer to move like an injured meal while staying in the protected waters of the river where large trout can safely feed.

TENSION NYMPHING

Problem: I'm having problems keeping my flies in the middle of the water column.

Solution: Try a tension drift with quick, last-minute adjustments.

While your line, leader, and indicator can be tension-free on the surface, the leader, tippet, and flies underwater may not be. Typically, they move with the water's current the same way a natural insect or food supply would. This has led me to use tension in most of my drifts so I can imitate a natural's movement while also having more control of my rig.

By supplying tension I can make a quick adjustment for distance by stripping in line. When the trout does take the fly, I can apply pressure faster with the hook set. Most importantly, with tension I can allow my flies to drift at different depths and enter the viewing lanes of suspended trout, which are often feeding.

With the addition of a Thingamabobber, I can now drift at a specific depth with tension and see the strike. While it is not as easy to see the take on a Thingamabobber compared to yarn, the pros far outweigh the cons. With yarn, you often see the indicator pause when a trout takes below the surface. With a Thingamabobber, a similar take would result in a sideways movement on the water's surface. Anglers need to pay attention to details during the drift no matter what indicator they are using.

Tension nymphing can be effective on stillwaters as well. With the wind making

Tim Christ displays the rewards of tension drifting with the wind on Eleven Mile Canyon Reservoir. The advantage to this method is being able to feel the slightest bump when big cruising trout take.

your flies drift sideways from shore, having tension will allow you to feel any takes when presenting in deep, dark, drop-off zones. With the addition of a mend or twitch, your flies can look like real, moving meals.

PRESENTING MICE

Problem: I don't know how to properly present mice.

Solution: Try creating a wake with your pattern if a drag-free drift is not working.

When a real mouse lands on the water's surface and survives, it moves like a dog paddling its feet, leaving a visible wake. The Morrish Mouse rides low on the surface, leaving a lifelike wake that attracts large trout.

When fishing drys—large imitations like mice in particular—it is easy to get caught up in the moment and simply watch your fly drift by on each cast.

Two common retrieves I see anglers use when fishing mice are popping the fly and twitching the fly in a skating imitation. These approaches can work, but they don't imitate the natural movements made by most mice in water.

When mice hit the water they commonly perform a dog-paddle motion in an effort to swim to safety while their tail wiggles to keep them in balance. From an angler's point of view the mouse causes a big V-wake as it moves to the bank. After countless hours of practice in mouse country (Alaska), I found the best way to mimic this: after a cast, with your rod tip just above the water's surface, slowly raise your rod to a vertical position with smooth acceleration. At an up- or downstream angle this will cause your fly to make a wake along the surface the way a real mouse does.

If the fish are not interested in movement, simply let the mouse drift like any other still dry. This is always the best backup plan because a dead food supply won't escape the fish. Alternatively, you can slap the pattern on the surface as you would a hopper, then allow the drag-free drift to draw the fish in to investigate an easy potential meal.

Lastly, target vegetation on the river's edge where it looks like a mouse could fall into the water. Tall patches of grass and wooded structure are great areas for mice to roam and at times slip to become a large trout meal.

WHEN IN DOUBT, SINK IT

Problem: The selective trout will not take my dry, even after trying numerous patterns and drifts.

Solution: Try riding your flies just below the surface film.

During my years guiding I have found that many anglers see the water's surface in two parts: above and below. While this is generally correct, there is a third part—the film—that is easily overlooked, and focusing your efforts here can eliminate the problem of catching selectively rising trout.

When trout are being selective while feeding on the surface, it is because they are wary of predators from above. And while their brains are only the size of a pea, their survival skills and adaptability can far exceed other animals'. Knowing that the fish is simply in survival mode, you want to trick the trout into believing it is eating in a safe zone—the film—where it does not have to break the surface and feed on top where predators are waiting. I always tell my clients when in doubt, sink your dry fly. Try sinking it one to four inches so it descends beyond the top of the surface to the film. The fish will still perform a rising motion visible to the angler, keeping its head just below the surface with its back bulging above.

There are two effective ways to sink your dry fly without going too deep. The first is to apply floatant to your leader and tippet, stopping a few inches above the first or main dry fly. This will keep the wet flies descending into the film and not below because the leader is floating. The second way is to use sinking materials while tying instead of using beaded flies or imitations with extra material that look unnatural. For example, if you were tying a dry fly with a dubbed thorax, you would normally use fine dry-fly dubbing. To sink the imitation naturally, you could replace the fine dry-fly dubbing with quick-descent dubbing that helps the flies get down to the safe zone.

KICK MENDING

Problem: I have trouble mending from an upstream position without spooking the trout

Solution: Kick mends downstream to extend an uninterrupted drift.

Habitually, we cast drys to rising trout from a downstream position. It is easier to see the presentation and set the hook, placing the flies in the corner of the fish's jaw. But it can be frustrating to watch pods of large rising trout be spooked by so many things from above: spraying water on the river's surface, glints of light off the fly line, shadows from the moving line, ticking the water's surface with your leader or flies—the list is endless.

I prefer to reverse my position and cast from upstream of the fish. Yes, there is more challenge in approach and positioning, but the reward is fewer spooked fish after each drift. To extend a drift beyond 15 feet with a conventional mend is tough because the moving line creates a disturbance on the water's surface. Instead, with your rod facing downstream after the cast and with the rod held just above water level, use a technique called the microsecond wrist. To do this, mimic the motion of an abstract artist holding a paint brush in his hand by pointing up with your elbow at your side and abruptly snapping the brush forward a few inches, as if spraying speckles of paint on the canvas. This same motion will shoot or throw line quickly, with fast energy moving from the wrist through the fly rod. With the microsecond wrist, kick any slack line that is hanging off your trigger finger by lifting the rod tip 12 inches, followed by an abrupt stop. Repeat this motion over and over, throwing loops of line downstream toward the target without disturbing the water or fish.

Not only will your drift be drag-free from the mends, it will also remain drag-free because the kicking mends are performed quickly. You can defeat an extremely fast current with multiple mends.

1. After the cast, position the rod tip just above the water's surface with enough slack line to feed downstream for a long drift. With the rod tip pointed at the fly line, pinch the line below the index finger of your casting hand while holding the slack line in your opposite hand. JAY NICHOLS PHOTOS

2. Use a microsecond wrist (see page 146) to quickly lift the rod tip one foot and immediately stop. This will start a loop positioned upward that will move forward toward the drift. At the same time you lift, quickly let go of the line below the index finger of your casting hand, and keep a loose hold of the fly line with your non-casting hand. Keep a soft grip with the non-casting hand so the line feeds forward and through the guides on the fly rod.

3. Once the loop begins moving forward, snap the rod tip back to the original starting position to kick out another mend. Keep the loose grip on the fly line with your non-casting hand, and do not grab the fly line with the index finger of your casting hand.

4. Repeat the same kick upward with the rod tip, forming another loop moving forward before the first loop collapses followed by snapping the rod tip back down.

5. Drop the rod tip to the original starting position. Repeat the kicks and snaps for mends until the slack line has moved through the rod's guides.

SHOOT MENDING

Problem: I am disturbing the water with my mend.

Solution: Shoot line above the water's surface when you mend with less disturbance.

A basic mend typically involves moving the rod tip in a half-circle motion and placing line upstream of your leader, flies, or indicator. This removes the tension applied to the rig by the moving current and helps you improve the depth and control of your presentation. The downside of the basic mend is how long it takes to perform and the water-disturbing movement it imparts to the fly or flies.

I have wonderful childhood memories of absorbing knowledge from the water or, during unfishable weather, watching instructional videos and reading every fishing book on the shelf over and over again. Doug Swisher is one of my idols and his Mastery Series videos with Scientific Anglers taught me great techniques that I still use today. In his video on selective trout, Doug demon-strated the stack mend, performed by throwing a mini-cast with a microsecond wrist and directing the line toward the flies or indicator. This will throw multiple quick loop "mends" on the water's surface, allowing you to get the ultimate drift and depth.

Years ago I started applying the same method with a sideways approach to replace the standard mend. I teach it to my clients with the term "shoot mending." By performing the same microsecond wrist cast with the tip of the rod moving forward only one foot, I turn the reel sideways in the direction I want the loop to unroll. Then, by quickly shooting one or two small mends, I can control a drift in a fraction of a second without moving the indicator or flies out of the trout's viewing lane.

1. After line lands on the water's surface in the direction of your presentation, elevate the rod to a position between nine and ten o'clock. This will create enough slack line below the rod to perform the mend. JAY NICHOLS PHOTOS

2. Use a microsecond wrist to kick the rod tip a few inches sideways in the opposite direction of the mend. This will load the rod with maximum flex without forcing you to move the rod downstream and take the flies out of the trout's feeding zone.

3. With power, kick the rod tip in a sideways motion one to two feet in the direction you want to mend, and then abruptly stop while keeping the rod positioned between nine and ten o'clock. The stored power will shoot a loop of line up- or downstream, similar to a casting stroke.

4. While the loop of line is traveling forward, keep the rod at between nine o'clock and ten o'clock to ensure there is no tension on the fly line from the water's surface.

5. Once the loop travels past the halfway point from the tip of the rod and the leader, begin dropping the rod toward the water's surface.

6. Keep the rod tip pointed at the fly or flies while you slowly drop the rod tip. This will prevent unnecessary drag on the fly line.

7. Complete the mend with your rod tip pointed at the leader just above the water's surface. You can shoot a mend in a matter of seconds, allowing a presentation that doesn't disturb the water's surface.

PIVOT NYMPHING

Problem: I keep missing the target while fishing multiple current speeds.

Solution: Try pivoting the drift of your leader from the position of the indicator.

When confronted with different speeds in a current over a larger casting distance, anglers attempt to adjust with too many mends or a tension drift that misses the target. To remedy this, use the indicator as a suspension tool in situations where the indicator is in slow-moving water while the tippet and flies are in faster water. I do this by casting up- or downstream at a 45-degree angle and allowing the indicator to land in a position where I know that the faster-moving water where the actual fly lands will pivot around the indicator, moving the fly directly into the trout's viewing lane.

When you're pivoting your flies, accuracy will change. Instead of looking at the location where the flies land on the surface, you should aim the indicator to a specific spot knowing that the leader and tippet will follow beyond the pivot location in the same straight line. This will help you locate various points in the river to pivot drift from for hard-to-reach trout.

While the indicator is stationary, you should visualize the fly or flies drifting downstream to the trout. I do this by moving my vision at the same speed as the river's current immediately after my flies break the water's surface. Often, the imitations move faster underwater than the water on the surface is moving. Be aware of any downstream movement from the trout even before you think the flies have reached the fish's viewing lane.

When faced with multiple current speeds it can be impossible to get an accurate conventional drift. If you use the indicator as a pivot position you can place it in the slow water, while your leader and flies drift to the target in the fast water. JOE MAHLER

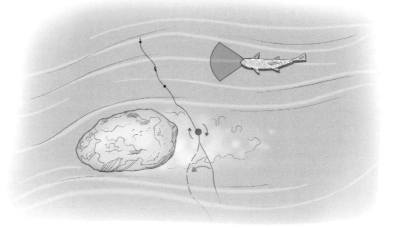

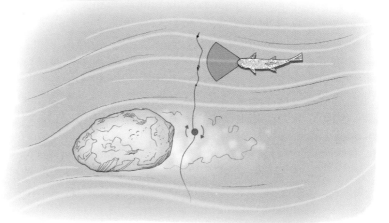

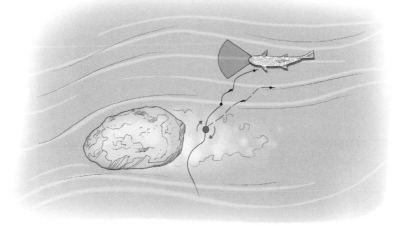

chapter NINE

Tough Landings

His name was Jim Parrist. Matt Bynum and I had guided him in Alaska. As our tip for that trip, Jim paid his captain in Florida to take us out for tarpon in Homosassa. In 2004, with dreams of the Mastery Series videos of Billy Pate landing tarpon at this location dancing in my head, Matt and I took Jim up on his generous offer. After traveling from historic Homosassa to Boca Grande during a five-day trip, I learned the value of applying maximum pressure without reaching the breaking point. The only way to accomplish this is by applying smooth acceleration and leverage to counterbalance the weight of a fish

You fight tarpon with the butt section of the rod using power generated from the legs up through the rod. This is leverage to keep power in place. The rod hardly ever reached a vertical position; it was always convex in front of me or to my side. This trip was where I truly learned what "breaking point" meant. This is vital because the fish has to constantly battle the pressure you apply during every minute of the battle.

I took that concept home and developed techniques for trout that allow you to land a 20-pound trout with only four to five pounds of pressure. Using the butt section—the strongest part of the fly rod—to apply power eliminated the need to use vertical lift during the fight and allowed my arm to become a shock absorber for powerful runs, jumps, and headshakes. I wish every trout fisher could experience tarpon at least once in his lifetime. If nothing else, it teaches you where fighting power really comes from and how to apply that power to land more fish.

HOOK-SET "LIFT"

Problem: I keep breaking off fish when setting the hook.

Solution: Elevate the rod by lifting to set when you see the take.

The first and last thirty seconds of the fight are when most trout are lost. I believe this happens because anglers have the tendency to lift vertically with the rod tip pointed up to twelve o'clock, break their wrist causing the rod tip to travel past the plane of the shoulder, or rotate their body causing the rod to drop back to two o'clock behind their shoulder. This forces the rod to reach maximum flex and applies all the power down to the tippet. This causes the rig to reach the breaking point.

Each position above, below, or across stream requires a specific rod position to set the hook. When you are above the fish, the challenge is to lift and put tension on the trout without pulling the fly out of its mouth. Any vertical lift from the rod pulls the fly away from the trout's jaw. You must be patient when the trout takes the fly and make sure you see that the fish has closed its mouth on the fly.

After the trout takes your fly, lift the rod at a 45-degree downstream angle or sideways, with the rod tip a foot or so above the water. Don't allow the rod tip to break the plane of your shoulder; once the tip has broken the imaginary line from your shoulder, the rod has reached its maximum flex and the trout will break off. This is what people refer to as the breaking point! For years I searched for the reason behind this. I finally realized it happens when the rod cannot flex any more and all the power is transferred to the tippet, causing it to break. To prevent this, when the trout begins to shake its head, bring your rod back to a vertical position. The fly will be in the corner of the trout's jaw, which is the best place to apply maximum tension and maintain control during the rest of the fight.

If you are below the trout, your hook set is more forgiving. The main objective is to elevate the rod to place the fly correctly. Remember that your goal after the set is to gain control: get to the river's edge and move upstream to prevent the fish from swimming upstream and finding structure or bolting downstream at you, causing the line to go slack.

Keep your rod pointed at eleven o'clock throughout the lift and raise your arm as you lift the rod. This keeps your rod high enough to get the proper tension on your line; your arm adds more length. By keeping the rod at eleven o'clock, you can drop the rod tip to adjust to a run when the trout begins to fight. To maximize the hook set, wait until the trout closes its mouth on the fly before you lift.

1. From either a low or high rod position, begin lifting the rod upward to 45-degrees at a downstream angle. The arm movement should be from your forearm, with your elbow tucked in toward your side. JAY NICHOLS PHOTOS

2. Continue the angle of this smooth acceleration while beginning to extend your arm for more pressure.

3. Once your rod tip reaches the plane of your shoulder, abruptly stop. From this position your arm can become a shock absorber for the trout's movement and prevent you from reaching the breaking point.

LINE CONTROL

Problem: I keep fumbling around with line during a fight and lose fish from slack and tangles.

Solution: Use your trigger finger and extended reach—not your hand—to control line.

Always practice line control during the fight by knowing where you can get a grip. I do this by using my peripheral vision and looking above the cork handle of the fly rod. This allows me to keep a visual on the trout and its movements. MARK ADAMS

Some fly fishers believe that stripping line again on the fish is the best method of keeping control. I don't believe this, but I admit that sometimes stripping in line is necessary to keep control of a trout that is moving toward you quickly. The challenge anglers face is fumbling line, or knowing where to reach and grab the line without hitting the opposite hand that is holding the rod.

I also used to grab line from my index finger or the cork handle of my rod. Often I lost trout by hitting my other hand when trying to grab line or by simply missing the line on a grab. I find it easier to grab line from above the handle or from the hand that is holding the rod. I prefer fighting trout with a convex bend in front of my body with my elbow down. This gives me more line for every strip, and I have more line to grab from my cork handle to my first guide on the rod, ensuring I will get line from every grab. After I grab new line from below the guide, I can then release line from below my index finger and reapply the index finger to the line during and after the next grab. You will gain three or four feet of line for every completed motion, compared with one or two feet from retrieving around your hand.

Do not attempt this technique with your rod above your head. It is impossible to see and you will have more control with your elbow down and the rod, line, and rod guides in front of you.

SAFE GAINS

Problem: The fish swim away so fast during the fight when I reel they often break off.

Solution: Try using three or four quick rotations with a pause between anticipating the next run.

Anglers often gain line during the fight by using a constant slow retrieve with no break in motion. With the trout generating so much explosive power during the fight, especially after the first initial run, it can be almost impossible to let go of the reel before the trout breaks off.

I always teach my clients to imagine the reel has been sitting on a piping hot stove: if you keep your fingers on the reel knob too long you will get burned. A safe and effective way to gain line during the fight is through three or four fast rotations, followed by a quick release of the reel. Anticipate a run so that when it does happen your hand is not on the reel, which can cause the trout to break off.

When you're gaining line with fast retrieves followed by quick pauses, try to always reel down to the fish with your rod remaining in a convex bend. This lets you gain more line on the trout and continue to apply maximum pressure during the fight, resulting in more control over the trout.

Lastly, get used to keeping your hand and fingers close to the reel during the fight without cupping or palming the reel face. This will train your hand to keep a safe distance and be ready to allow the trout to run near the end of the fight with one last burst of speed.

Richard Cota reels up on a quality brown on the South Platte River. By slowly lowering his flexed rod when gaining on the trout, he had more short line control to lift the fish's head.

HEADSHAKES

Problem: My rig is wrapping around the trout during the fight and breaking off.

Solution: Try placing your rod at a 45-degree angle upstream during headshakes.

The key to preventing breakoffs by large trout is always making adjustments with the rod angle and pressure in reaction to the trout's aggressive movements.

When you hook a large trout, the fish will often wrap the rig or trailing flies around its body. A large trout's headshakes can be so aggressive that its head is almost touching its tail, forming a donut appearance.

The proper rod placement during the fight is at a 45-degree and downstream angle. But leaving the rod at this position during the headshakes will increase the chance of the fish rolling up on the rig. Instead, when you see or feel the target beginning to headshake, quickly move and place the rod at an 11 o'clock upstream position. This will move the lead or trailing fly, leader, and tippet upstream of the shaking body and prevent snags and breakoffs. Once the trout has returned to a holding or swimming body position facing upstream, reposition the rod to a downstream angle. You can do the reverse if the target is moving downstream, headshaking while performing a powerful run. In this situation you would reposition the rod to 1 o'clock during the shakes.

When performing these angles make the movements of the rod tip smooth. If you move too fast and apply to much thrusting force you can wear the fly loose in the trout's mouth. Even if you cannot see the fish, the technique can be performed by feel when the rod thumps from the power in each shake.

SETTING ON THE TROUT'S MOVEMENTS

Problem: I keep foul-hooking fish when I set after seeing them move.

Solution: Watch and wait for a fish to straighten back out before setting the hook.

Most set the hook when the trout moves to feed or when the fly or flies are in the vicinity of the fish. While this can be effective, you may foul-hook trout or lose them after only a few seconds of fighting because the fly has barely penetrated the outside corner of the fish's jaw.

When trout feed, they move with their mouths open, ready to consume the meal. Once they have the meal in their mouths, they straighten their bodies out while closing their mouths at the same time. Their gills flare out and create suction in conjunction with the open mouth. By watching and waiting to set until the fish is straight in a natural holding position below the surface, you will stop the headshakes from setting on the move. The fly will then penetrate the corner of the fish's jaw, ensuring the fight will be on. The imitation will stay in place in the jaw, eliminating the possibility of foul-hooking the fish.

Determine how the fish is moving to find out which set will work the best. Some are feeding by moving side to side, while others are lifting. Make sure that they are actually feeding and not simply avoiding something, or being territorial against other fish. Observe the fish's behavior first and then present and set accordingly.

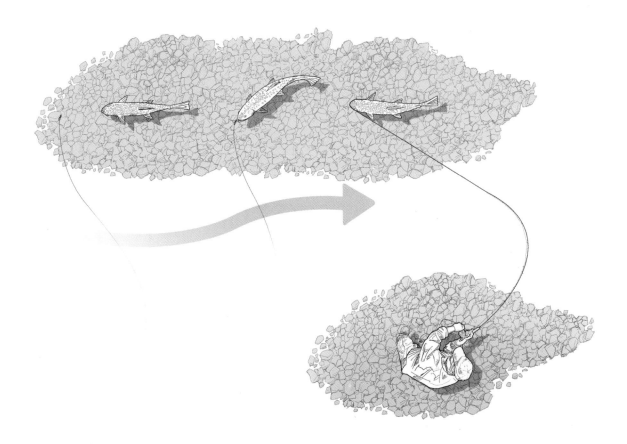

1. When the trout first spots a food supply, it will hesitate for a split second. Sometimes it will drift backwards to investigate the potential meal.
2. By moving to one side, or lifting in the water column, the trout will curve its body to take the imitation. This means the trout's mouth is open while it feeds. Do not set while the trout has a curved body.
3. After the fish takes, it will go back to a straight-profile body with its mouth closed. This is when you want to set by lifting at a downstream angle. JOE MAHLER

CONVEXLY

Problem: I keep lifting my rod vertically during the fight and breaking off fish.

Solution: Elevate your arm and rod while maintaining a convex bend.

Some trout are simply too strong for the size of tippet you're using. To avoid breaking off, point the tip of the rod at the trout when it runs, forming a convex bend. This applies maximum pressure from the butt section of the rod while letting the reel do its job.

Many images from our sport's past feature an angler fighting a trout with the tip of the rod straight up in the air and with arms fully extended. Such images are a guide's worst enemy because we constantly have to correct this bad form from our clients. A vertical lift is not the answer for quickly getting a trout to the net because there is not enough lifting power in that particular tip section of the rod.

Instead, lift while performing a convex bend with the rod. This applies lifting power from the butt section—the strongest portion of the rod. Most anglers lose trout in the first or last thirty seconds of the fight by applying the wrong amount of power. For example, if you apply a smooth lift when the trout eats and reel down to maintain the convex bend, you can adjust if the trout runs away from you without reaching the breaking point by pointing your rod straight at the trout. This lets the high-end drag on the reel do its job. Then, when the fish bolts back toward you, as many trout do, lift to a vertical position without losing tension during the fight. If your rod were vertical, it would reach the breaking point, and the trout's bolt back to the bank would cause your line to go limp.

By using a convex bend, you can move up- and downstream with all of your tools in front of you. With the trout in your direct vision, the reel, line, and entire rod fall in your peripheral vision. This way you don't have to move your head to coordinate landing the fish.

A BATTLESHIP WITH FINS

Problem: I am having trouble fighting and netting fish from a belly boat.

Solution: Try moving in half circles with your fins below the surface of the water for proper rotation.

Fighting trout while sitting water-level in a belly boat can be one of the most exciting angling experiences. You'll feel the surface disturbance created by the trout's headshakes up close and personal, and you may even see the fish jumping higher than your head. The problem you'll face is in keeping up with the fish when they run and netting the trout when it's close enough. It can be overwhelming doing this when you're in a moving boat in the river.

Fish in stillwaters run because they're fast and always moving to search for their next meal. To keep close tension on trout while in a belly boat or float tube, think reverse. With your right or left leg, move the boat in a half circle with your fin pointed straight down once the fish begins to run. This will im-mediately turn your back toward the running trout and allow you to kick backward toward the fish. This puts the boat in the best aerodynamic position, allowing you to move faster. Keep your feet and fins just below the surface in front of you, lifting and dropping each foot separately in short, quick kicks. This will increase your speed while moving you backward. When you're in motion, keep the rod up at a twelve o'clock or eleven o'clock position while looking over your shoulder. Once you see the fish stop running or your line slackens, perform another half-circle kick with one leg to turn you into position to face the fish and gain line. This keeps you from losing trout to long line release as they run far and drop in the weeds.

When netting a trout from the boat, I prefer to net from the side of my craft. It is easier to lean to the side for extension with your netting hand than it is from straight forward or behind. You will find yourself turning, sometimes in circles, when the end of the fight is near and the trout does some last-second dives to get free. Just like when you turned the boat when the fish was swimming, rotate one leg in a half circle while your other foot and fin is lifted back so that it almost touches your butt. This creates fewer objects for the leader or tippet to wrap around as the fish speeds under you. You can then turn on a dime and reposition to have the fish at your side and ready for the net.

If you kick away from the trout in a watercraft you can make sure the fish will not dart below the boat, and help maintain flex in the rod to prevent the fish from spitting out your fly.
JAY NICHOLS

ONCE YOU GO SLACK YOU NEVER GO BACK

Problem: I am having problems landing trout around structure.

Solution: Try allowing your line to go slack while the trout moves around the structure.

When battling trout around structure, some keep constant pressure from a downstream angle, causing the leader or tippet to break around rocks or logjams.

To avoid this, when the trout moves around the structure, keep the rod at an upstream angle to dictate which direction the fish will take. Then use the tip of the rod as an extension to guide the line, leader, and fish around the structure and prevent breakage. Once the fish has cleared the structure, bring the rod back to a downstream angle and continue the fight.

Trout move downstream or toward structure to relieve themselves of the pressure of the fight. Drop your rod tip and allow the line to go slack as the fish is moving around the structure. This relieves the pressure that the fish feels, causing it to stop running and hold its position. As you strip in the slack, you can then use the tip of your rod to guide the line, leader, and tippet around the structure. Once the line is clear of the structure, reapply pressure and continue the fight.

While fighting trout around rocks, look at more than just the rock the trout is currently moving around. Even before casting, look downstream to all of the obstacles ahead and find an alley between and around the structures that leads to a point where you can properly net the fish.

The problem with fighting trout in these areas is that anglers try to pull the fish away from the structure or against the heavy current. Sometimes you can get the trout to turn in your favor and bring it to the river's edge, but most of the time you will lose this fight because the rod has reached maximum flex and the pressure transfers to the tippet, causing it to break. When trout are moving out of control downstream, or around structure, drop your rod tip directly in front of you and start to gain line by reeling in the slack line. Reposition yourself directly across from the trout or across from the structure where the fish is, reapply tension, and begin to fight the trout with the tip and fly line clear of any objects or fast currents. Trout will stop running when they no longer feel pressure in the corner of their jaw. This is why you can catch up to the fish and begin the fight again, remaining in control and without losing the fish.

1. When the trout moves around the structure, keep slight pressure on the rod tip by applying a partial bend. MICHELLE MAYER PHOTOS

2. Immediately grab the line from the back of the reel with your non-casting hand and extend your arm straight downstream, pulling out three to four feet.

3. Point the rod tip directly at the fly line and the top of the structure, causing the line in the water and your hand to go slack. Make sure the rod tip is positioned just past the structure so that you can clear line. Allow the current to pull slack line out of your non-casting hand by keeping a loose grip on the line. Continue to follow the moving slack line.

4. Once the loose line begins to drift downstream and clear the structure, start to lift the rod slowly at a downstream angle. Continue to keep a loose grip on the fly line in your non-casting hand.

5. When the fly line is completely clear downstream of the structure, apply a maximum convex bend with the rod and continue the fight while moving downstream.

MOVING FIGHT

Problem: I keep breaking off fish when trying to move them toward the bank from a stationary position.

Solution: Move with the fish until you are perpendicular to it to achieve maximum pressure.

When fishing in turbulent water, take one step at a time or use the buddy system, as Sharon Lance does here amid the swift currents of American Creek in Alaska. While you are moving, point the rod in the direction of the fast-moving target and allow the pressure from the reel's drag to keep the fly in place. MARK LANCE

During the fight with a fish, anglers often try to pull the trout toward the bank they're standing on by applying maximum pressure when the fish is on the move.

This will cause many breakoffs that can be avoided by adjusting to the movement.

You have no control when trout are on the move during the fight. To prevent the trout from breaking off after the fish has moved up- or downstream, you must move your body to catch up with the fish. Once you have reached the trout, position yourself across from or perpendicular to the fish with the rod bent at a downstream angle.

If you can't move your body fast enough during the fight to remain perpendicular to the trout, place your rod tip directly downstream to maintain sideways pressure until you can catch up and continue moving with the fight.

NETTING LARGE FISH

Problem: I am having trouble getting fish into the net without breaking them off.

Solution: Net the fish headfirst, or use an extended handle to net the fish when they are off-balance.

Anglers lose most trout in the first or last thirty seconds of the fight because they use too much power, which causes the fish to break off or spit out the hook. When fly fishers see the trout at the end of the fight, they get anxious and often try to net the fish too soon when the fish is tailfirst. To overcome this problem, pay attention to the movement of the target, and time when you go in with the net.

Always net the trout headfirst. The best way to do this is to sight-fish during the fight. You will see when the trout is on the surface and off-balance as it performs aggressive headshakes and body thrashes. If the trout is upside down during those movements it will take the fish a few seconds to gain its balance, opening a window for you

to net the fish headfirst. This way, if the trout does bolt away, it will continue to drive its body into the net. A second way to ensure the net is in front of the fish's head is to make sure the trout is off-balance and facing upstream at the end of the fight. You can then net the trout headfirst by sliding the net opening below the trout. Once the basket's opening is upstream of the fish, lift up the front of the net to ensure a headfirst scoop. Always use a longer reach with an extended net handle when netting the fish. Instead of arching your back to pull the target in, lift your rod arm up and behind you at a 45-degree angle. Then reach out with the net hand to give yourself four or five inches more reach than you'd have in a standard netting position. This is a great approach

When trout are off-balance and facing upstream at the end of the fight, you can net the trout headfirst by sliding the net opening below the trout. Once the basket's opening is upstream of the fish, lift up the front of the net to ensure a headfirst scoop. ANGUS DRUMMOND

because even if the trout bolts during the fight you can return to a normal stance with the rod in front to fight the trout.

When possible, lead the trout downstream and allow the current to drift the fish into the net. You can net from above the trout, but these fish are notorious for drifting with the current and using the power of the water during the fight.

UPSTREAM

Problem: I am having problems fighting a fish and keeping line control from an upstream position.

Solution: Try applying pressure from an upstream angle to force the fish to move toward you to relieve pressure.

The rod tip should be placed in line with the trout's head when fighting trout from an upstream position. The fish will swim toward you to relieve the pressure it feels on its jaw. MARK LANCE

When anglers fight trout from an upstream position without the chance to move downstream, they tend to maintain sideways pressure, which causes the fish to bolt downstream and break off.

Keep the rod tip directly upstream of the trout or, if possible, wade out to where you can position yourself upstream of the trout with your rod flexed with a convex bend. It may be an awkward angle, but it will cause the trout to swim upstream toward you in an attempt to relieve the pressure on its jaw. Then, when the fish is close enough, you can quickly apply sideways pressure to move the target to the river's edge for netting. If the trout begins to fight or dart downstream again, repeat the process by reapplying the upstream pressure. If the fish simply will not stop running downstream, try placing the tip and upper portion of the rod down directly into the water. Then, with smooth rotations, begin reeling in the taut line. Be prepared to let go of the reel if the fish does a sudden bolting run. This straight plane pressure upstream of the trout can cause the fish to swim back to the position of the bank you are standing on to relieve the pressure in its jaw. This will give you a chance to gain line and control of the fish.

ROLLING OVER STRUCTURE

Problem: I keep breaking fish off while trying to keep them moving around structure.

Solution: Use slack line during the fight and roll-cast over the structure to keep your rig clear of hazards.

Some fish are simply too strong and fast for us to react to when they bolt around structure from a distance. Many anglers react by reeling and applying too much pressure, hoping the trout will backtrack around the structure point. The leader and tippet will simply break from rubbing against the structure's rough surface.

When you are too far away from the structure to guide the line, drop your tip to allow the line to go slack and then pull two or three feet of slack line off the reel. Then bring your rod to a vertical position and roll-cast over the structure. The motion should be faster and shorter than a normal roll cast because you have to perform the act quickly. From a twelve o'clock or eleven o'clock position, perform a fast forward cast (push), aiming the tip of the rod above the rock or log structure. This will allow the forward loop enough clearance to roll over the obstacle. When the line clears reapply pressure to continue the fight from a downstream angle.

1. When the fish moves around structure, maintain pressure while dropping the rod tip in the direction you're pointing, slightly upstream of the object. MICHELLE MAYER PHOTOS

2. With your free hand that isn't holding the rod, strip out two or three feet of slack line from the back of the reel opening. Make sure you maintain only a slight bend in the tip of the rod to prevent breaking off.

3. Once you pull out enough slack, let go of the line and begin lifting the rod to a ten o'clock sideways angle without applying pressure on the rod tip. Having the rod at a sidearm position will give you enough distance to push forward in the cast. Use the slack line to roll over the structure.

4. From the sidearm ten o'clock position, push forward two or three feet with the tip of the rod pointed one or two feet above the structure; then abruptly stop.

5. Hold the rod position above the structure while a loop of line is rolling above and over the structure.

6. Travel downstream with the tip of the rod pointed at the loop that is clearing the structure. Once everything is clear you can then lift up at a downstream angle and continue the fight.

REELING WITHOUT A HANDLE

Problem: I keep missing my reel handle or line during the fight and the fish gets away.

Solution: Gain line during the fight without using the reel handle.

In the heat of battle, it can be difficult to find the reel handle because all your attention is focused on the trout, as it should be. As with knot-tying sequences, the key is finding a way to perform by feel rather than sight when you are locked in on a fish. This is especially true during the fight, when you must adjust to every move the trout makes.

This technique came to me after several guide trips with clients who were used to stripping in line while fighting the fish. Gaining line from each strip was not the problem; it was when the fish did not take back the slack line that things went wrong. Taking your eyes off the battling trout to look at the reel was difficult. And you have to consider the possibility of the loop of line shooting up in the air and wrapping around the reel frame, causing the trout to break off.

Using your index and middle fingers—without your thumb—mimic the motion of snapping your fingers with the index and middle finger on the rim of the reel face. This will quickly spin the face and allow you to gain several feet of line with each snap. The great part is with a little practice, you can do it all by feel. This technique is also effective when presenting flies if you have to adjust the cast and it leaves you with slack line off the reel that you don't need.

1. Position your free hand a finger's length away from the rim of the reel.

JAY NICHOLS PHOTOS

2. Place your middle and index fingers on the edge of the reel's rim near the cork handle of the fly rod. Tuck your ring and pinky fingers out of the way near the palm of your hand.

3. Use force to push straight down on the face with your thumb, middle, and index fingers. Mimic the speed you would use to snap your fingers.

4. Allow the reel to move forward and freely gain line. Concentrate on the trout; you will know the slack line is gone by the sound the reel makes when it comes to an abrupt stop. You can repeat the motion numerous times to gain multiple feet of line.

Tying Flies

Mayer's Mini Leech

Leeches are an important part of a trout's diet, especially in high-water conditions. Similar to worms, leeches are swept off the river's edge and bottom, supplying an easy food supply for the fish. While some leeches are large, exceeding one inch, there are just as many that are less than an inch long, making the common two- to three-inch leech patterns ineffective at times. I designed the Mayer's Mini Leech to match the small freshwater leeches that trout feed on in rivers and stillwaters. Read more about this pattern in the "Leech Lesson" tip on page 6.

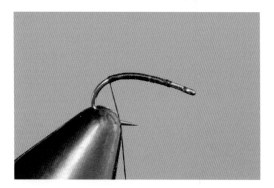

1. Start a hook point's length behind the eye of the hook and wrap a clean thread base to the bend of the hook using black 8/0 UNI thread.

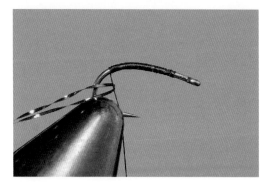

2. Take one strain of black Krystal Flash and fold it over the thread at the bend of the hook.

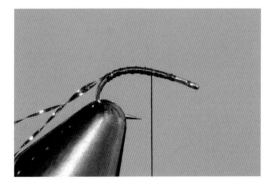

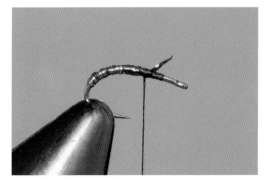

3. Lift the thread and bobbin above the hook shank, sliding the Krystal Flash down the bend of the hook. Perform two secure wraps back toward the bend to secure the Flash in place. Then continue wrapping the thread forward toward the eye of the hook and stop halfway on the shank of the hook.

5. Cut the flash tag ends, leaving enough length to help build the head of the leech later in the tying sequence.

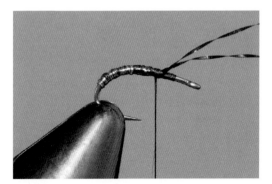

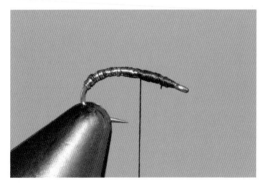

6. Wrap the thread forward and back once to create an even and level thread base.

4. With the thumb and index finger of your dominant hand, grab the two tag ends of Krystal Flash and begin wrapping it forward. With your opposite thumb and index finger, grab the two tag ends of Flash halfway into each wrap. Trading fingers will ensure the Krystal Flash lays evenly over the thread base. When you reach the stopping point of the thread, place two secure wraps to keep the flash in place.

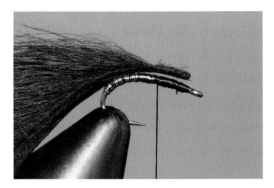

7. Cut a piece of micro pine squirrel to twice the length of the hook shank. Hold the strip of squirrel above the hook shank to determine the length of the thread base behind the eye of the hook. Strip off the same length of micro pine squirrel from the skin to allow a smooth connection to the hook shank.

9. At the end of the thread base next to the micro pine squirrel, place a single piece of ostrich herl the same color as the squirrel at a 45-degree angle. As you did with the squirrel skin, clean a small section of the ostrich herl's spine to allow a smooth connection on the thread base. Wrap the thread forward, stopping behind the eye of the hook.

8. Using one loose wrap, secure the clean squirrel skin to the hook shank with even wraps of thread. Make sure the skin lays flat to prevent it from rotating.

10. Trading off the thumb and index fingers of both hands, carefully perform three even wraps forward, stopping at the eye of the hook. Hold the herl in place and perform two secure wraps of thread to keep it there.

11. Cut the herl close to the eye of the hook. Using your whip-finish or fingers secure three wraps to build a head and perform proper knots.

13. The finished black Mayer's Mini Leech.

12. Perform two whip-finish knots to secure the leech.

Mayer's *Mysis*

Born and raised in Colorado, my addiction for hunting trophy trout lasted through all four seasons, especially on the tailwaters of the Taylor, Frying Pan, and the Blue Rivers. These *Mysis* drainages force you to evaluate your patterns on a regular basis, trying to find the creation that works in both high- and low-water conditions. My *Mysis* evolved ten years ago after I noticed that you need natural movement from the fly to imitate the natural movement of live shrimp as well as the shrimp that are shredded and dead. In addition, you want a fly that can match the translucent look of a live *Mysis* and the opaque color of a dead *Mysis*. With clear rubber antennae and a white ostrich thorax, this imitation will pulsate in any current speed while maintaining flash, with the tinsel on the thorax and abdomen capturing the attention of the large trout.

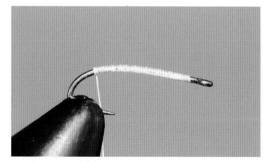

1. Start behind the eye of the hook and build an even thread base back toward the bend using white 8/0 UNI thread.

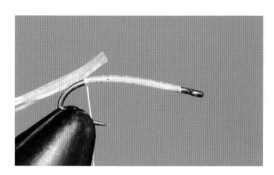

2. Place five strains of clear tentacle legs on the thread base at the bend of the hook.

3. Wrap an even thread base over the tentacles to secure them in place. The tentacles' tag ends and thread base should be a hook point in length.

4. Start at the middle of the new thread base and place a one-inch piece of black rubber leg with a loose wrap.

5. Perform three or four figure-eight wraps to secure the eyes in place. Make adjustments with your fingers when needed to keep the eyes horizontal and even.

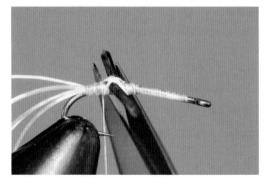

6. Cut the eyes close to the hook shank to mimic the eyes of a natural shrimp. This will make it easier to apply other materials to the fly as well.

7. Cut a tag end in the shape of an arrow using a one-inch strip of medium Mylar tinsel. This will ensure the tinsel lays evenly behind the black rubber leg eyes without rotating when you secure it down. Use loose wraps to secure the tinsel down, with the point of the tinsel arrow placed in between the black eyes. Wrap the thread back to the starting point of the thread base at the bend of the hook. Place a two-inch piece of white ostrich herl, with a clean spine on one tag end, on the bend of the hook at a 45-degree angle.

8. Use one loose wrap and one tight wrap to secure the herl with the thread.

9. Use your thumb and index fingers on both hands to rotate the ostrich herl forward, trading off fingers with each rotation for even proportioning. Continue wrapping forward two rotations past the black eyes and secure it with the thread.

11. Secure the herl with two tight wraps of thread to ensure it stays in place.

10. Cut the tag end of herl close to the shank of the hook.

12. Continue wrapping the thread forward to the eye of the hook and then stop.

13. Wrap the thread back toward the bend of the hook, stopping at the ostrich herl. If need be you can supply additional wraps to clean up loose herl on the hook shank.

14. Pull the Mylar tinsel forward over the ostrich herl and the black eyes. Make sure the tinsel lies flat on the hook shank and secure it with one loose and two tight wraps of thread.

16. Place two even tight wraps at the eye of the hook to keep the Mylar tinsel in place. Grab the long tag end of tinsel and pull it back to allow room for a whip-finish knot behind the eye of the hook. Perform two whip-finish knots in front of the Mylar tinsel behind the eye of the hook.

15. Continue forward with separated loose wraps of thread over the Mylar tinsel to the eye of the hook. If needed, adjust the tinsel after each loose wrap to make sure it is placed evenly on the hook shank.

17. Cut the thread close to the eye of the hook. Pull the Mylar tinsel forward over the eye of the hook and cut, leaving a quarter-inch tag end.

18. Cut the tentacle antennae to half a hook shank in length.

19. The finished Mayer's *Mysis*.

Tube Midge

As a full-time guide, you quickly realize how important segmentation and durability in midge imitations are. When you see midges in the water or pull them out of the seine, it looks like the life of the insect is encased in a clear, ribbed body. I tried to match this effect with Ultra Wire inserted into clear tubing before wrapping it on the hook shank. Not only does it give the midge a clear, natural appearance, but it also makes the fly incredibly durable, helping it perform well on more than one fish. With white, egg-veil gills, this pattern has worked well for me and for my clients over the years.

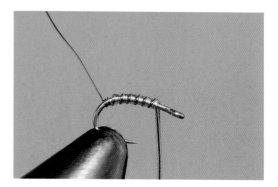

2. With your dominant index and thumb fingers, pinch the wire and tubing and evenly wrap three quarters of the way to the eye of the hook. Be sure to leave space for a thread head behind the eye of the hook. Simply let go of the wire and tubing; the materials will hold in place.

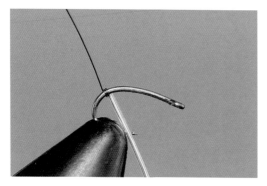

1. Perform two wraps with small Ultra Wire at the bend of the hook shank. Then slide a one-and-a-half-inch piece of clear micro tubing onto the tag end of the wire closest to the eye of the hook.

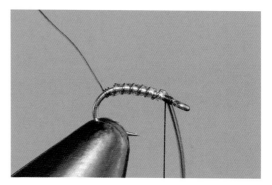

3. Starting behind the eye of the hook, make six wraps of black 8/0 UNI thread toward the bend of the hook. Remove the tag end of the thread by pulling abruptly for a clean break.

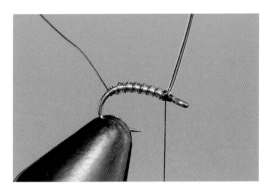

4. Hold the tubing and wire tag end and place three secure wraps to keep the wire and tubing in place.

7. Starting behind the tag end of wire and tubing, wrap forward and back once to cover the tag end. This will build a nice oval-shaped head.

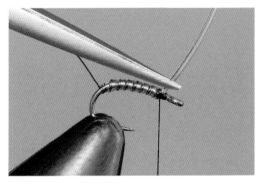

5. Cut the wire and tubing as close to the hook shank as possible.

8. Twist a one-inch piece of egg veil yarn in your fingers to form a rope. Fold the rope of egg veil over the thread and place it at the back end of the thread head.

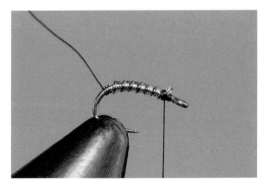

6. The leftover short tag will help build a head under the thread base.

9. Lift the black thread with the bobbin above the thread of the fly. With your opposite thumb and index fingers, slide the rope of egg veil down to the thread on the head. Perform one cinch wrap to secure the egg veil.

11. Let the bobbin hang down with the thread in place and cut the long tag end of the egg veil the length you want for imitating the midge's antennae. I leave mine long, allowing me to cut and make length adjustments on the water.

10. Wrap the thread forward evenly to cover the egg veil on the head of the midge.

12. Use a whip-finish tool or your fingers to secure the thread head with two knots and cut it off with your scissors.

13. With your dominant thumb and index fingers, grab the tag end of wire at the back of the hook. Rotate the wire in a small circle while you pull it toward the eye of the hook. This will give you a clean break and look at the bend of the hook. Lastly, place a dab of superglue for added durability.

14. The finished red Tube Midge.

Afterword

While I am blessed to be able to make a living fly fishing, the true blessing is being able to learn from the entire picture. When you are fishing, your concentration is typically on the presentation, the water, and the fish. As a guide you are able see the whole picture of the fish, the water, the hatch, and the angler and the presentation— all the motions are in one scene. This has allowed me to fine-tune the details of body movement, positioning, battle sequences, presentations, and beyond. This further developed my ability to teach the details and offer clients the fine-tuning all anglers need to improve their skills.

A lot of the tips in this book are a result of being able to dissect what I am seeing on a daily basis. And the photographic teachings are the same images that I have used to zero in on the good and the bad, all motions in one scene. I hope that reading this book has helped build your visual confidence. Fly fishing does not stop after you leave the water. As the day's trip runs through my head at night, I am visualizing key moments of what went right and what went wrong, leading me to decide what I am going to do differently the next day, or how I am going to make something good even better. I am fly fishing by imagining the events in my mind. This makes our great sport an affair that continues even after I go home.

I truly hope that this book supplies anglers with the same tools that I use on a daily basis. In addition to introducing you to a wide variety of methods, both conventional and unconventional, these tips can help keep trout in your local waterway feeling less pressure because many of them are designed to give anglers a stealthier presence. With the sport of fly fishing becoming increasingly popular in this age of instant fishing reports and photos of the day's catch zoomed across the world at the speed of light, it has become all the more important for the future of our great sport that we keep our fish healthy and happy. We only get one shot at this life and every trout and angler counts.

Tight Lines,
Landon Mayer

Index

Page numbers in italics indicate photos.